Elizabeth's Lives & Times

Elizabeth Howard

Copyright © 2025 Elizabeth Howard
All Rights Reserved

 Year of the Book
135 Glen Avenue
Glen Rock, PA 17327

ISBN: 978-1-64649-496-5 (paperback)
ISBN: 978-1-64649-497-2 (ebook)

No part of this publication may be reproduced, distributed, or transmitted in any form or by any means, including photocopying, recording, or other electronic or mechanical methods, without the prior written permission of the publisher, except as permitted by U.S. copyright law.

This book is memoir. It reflects the author's present recollections of experiences over time. Some names and characteristics have been changed, some events have been compressed, and some dialogue has been recreated.

A Letter to Connor

Age 16

Connor, I am counting on you, the oldest of my great grandchildren, to share my memories with your siblings and cousins when they are old enough to care about midcentury life in Texas. When I was young, I seldom thought about the people in my family who had gone ahead of me. I was acquainted with three of my grandparents, but I looked right through them, as though they were irrelevant to my life.

This account begins with an idea which occurred to me when I found a wedding photo of my great grandmother in a closet after my mother died in 1983. Laura Ellen Taylor was born in Winnsboro, Texas, in 1856, some ten years after Texas joined the United States. There is talk in the family she was related to Zachary Taylor, the twelfth President and hero of the Texas-Mexican War, but my interest in her lies in her beauty, not her lineage. Laura Ellen was stunning, not stiff looking and severe like the people in most old photographs. Her hair was piled on the top of her head, her skin flawless.

Now, thirty-nine years later, at age eighty, I try to imagine what her life was like in a world before terrorist attacks in the East and wildfires in the West, before climate change and the destruction of the World Trade Center, and before Antarctica's glaciers melted. What were her fears and hopes, her goals, habits? What did people call her? Laura Ellen or a nickname? Sadly, I can't know much.

Laura Ellen lived before cars and good roads and supermarkets. Her generation knew nothing of air travel or space exploration. The list goes on: air conditioning, indoor plumbing, electric lights, and developments she and those around her could not even dream about.

That thought brings me to the present day, my own children, and my present attempt to portray for them an account of what my life was like "in the olden days." Occasionally I appeared to wander away from sanity, but it took every day I lived, every success and failure to bring me to this most serene point in my life. I don't want "my kids" to make the same mistakes I made, and I invite all of you to analyze what I did and thought and, if necessary, what I should have done and thought instead.

I love my descendent family and, as a lifelong teacher, I hope you all learn to skip my pitfalls and live a happy, productive life. I commit this effort, turning a new page on the golden rule: I am doing for my descendants what I wish my ancestors had done for me, offering an account of my own life and times.

The Beginning

My mother, Enna Mitchell, married my father on Christmas Day 1930, during the Great Depression, a time when jobs were few and pay was low. At my advanced age today, I look back on my parents with amazement. Richard Crawford, my father, owned a drug store before World War II interrupted everybody's life; my mother, Enna, was a housewife. Together they created a safe bubble for me to grow up in. Unaware of the war, I feared only the danger to be found at the end of my mother's patience. When she got tired or didn't feel good, I was usually in trouble.

When I was very young, before Mama's threats to kill me started, I felt like the luckiest girl in the world. I was loved and secure, especially when I was with her.

Our family numbered four people: Mama, Daddy, my sister Enna Frances, born in 1931, and me. My birth date is November 23, 1939, Franksgiving Day, a popular name for the Thanksgiving President Franklin Roosevelt moved up a week earlier to give merchants more time to prepare for Christmas sales.

Like Okies during the 1930s dustbowl, my family left Texas early in the war and moved to California looking for jobs. My father's pitifully flat feet rendered him 4F, exempt, in the draft. The year was 1942, America's first complete year of the war. He and my mother found work in the construction of battleships and aircraft carriers in Richmond; Enna Frances went to school; and I stayed in our apartment with Biggie, my maternal grandmother. Daddy worked as a pipe fitter and welder, skills he learned quickly and used for years instead of pharmacy because of construction's bigger paychecks. Mama worked in an office.

I recall a few snippets of our lives in California: my fourth birthday and the morning after a series of tremors danced our piano to the middle of the living room. Some incidents stamped themselves on my early memory because of strong emotion generated by me or family members. My introduction to castor oil occurred in California. When my daddy put a spoonful in my mouth, my stomach immediately rejected it. I don't remember the reason for the castor oil, only the horrible taste and vomiting. He slapped me hard across the face and demanded I keep the castor oil in my stomach. I kept it down the second time.

Joe and Caroline McCasland, Mama's sister and her husband, and their daughter Jo Carol also went to Northern California. Uncle Joe, our most flamboyant relative, served as a government lawyer in San Francisco. He drove a new Buick convertible in which our family toured on weekends. Jo Carol was eight days older than my sister, both of them old enough to be fish bigger than me in my food chain.

The Piney Woods of East Texas

Shortly after victory in Europe, VE Day, in April 1945, our family returned to East Texas, leaving to others the job of wrapping war things up. We went first to Jefferson, where Uncle Joe and Aunt Caroline owned an antebellum home. As a small child, I thought it was huge. As an adult, I'm surprised it looks like a normal two-story with columns.

The house was in a state of flux, even its location. Some men came and loaded it onto big flat-bed trailers and repositioned it back from the street to the middle of the two adjacent lots. The upstairs remained almost untouched, but the first floor was gutted. A makeshift kitchen on the second floor served until the original one downstairs could be fitted with plumbing and new appliances. We all slept upstairs in several bedrooms.

A creaky stepladder led up into a spooky attic, where my two cousins, Jo Carol and Wilma Jean, and my sister Fran, ages eleven, eight, and eleven respectively, often turned the light off, lay in wait, and made woo-woo ghost sounds in the dark when I found them. I screamed, and my mama practically flew up the ladder to get to me, yelling at the older girls to stop scaring her baby.

Connor, today the Captain's Castle is a bed and breakfast inn. Jefferson has become quite a tourist spot. Sally and I spent two nights there a few years ago when we attended Jefferson's Christmas parade of homes. At breakfast, I related to the other guests how it was to live there. Jo Carol's picture still graces the entry, and a short bio of Judge Joe McCasland, Uncle Joe, hangs under it.

Mama's family, her mother and four siblings, lived in East Texas. The Red River flows from the Texas Panhandle east to the

Oklahoma, Arkansas, and Louisiana borders. Mom's sister Mary Lou and her family, lived in Talco, her brother Dan and his family in Mount Pleasant, and Biggie, my grandmother, in Avinger. Those towns were north, along the jagged border where Arkansas meets Texas on the northeast corner. Caroline, the oldest of the five, lived with her family in Jefferson. David Emmitt, Mama's brother, lived in Marshall. Both towns are close to the Louisiana border.

On weekend visits to Aunt Mary Lou in Talco, northwest of Jefferson, I joined Wilma Jean in playing games she created. We took scarves and fabric into the woods and designed beautiful clothes, wrapping the fabrics around our bodies, walking around like high fashion models. Another activity was "Adventuring."

At that time and unlike today, East Texas was almost solid forest. A few little towns dotted the landscape, but cities, like Dallas, were over 100 miles away. Talco is in the East Texas Oil Field, and oil production was about the only industry.

On one of our adventures, Jean and I took lunch in a basket and went exploring. We walked through the woods, finding sweet gum trees with delicious sap to chew along the way. She knew myriad things to do in the woods, so I mostly followed her lead. I was scared of bears, but she assured me Theodore Roosevelt and his friends had killed all of Texas' bears.

Jean found a slush pit, a big, deep hole in the ground where trash oil was discarded. We took sticks and poked at the thick, black sludge. At one point, I got too close, and my feet began to slide toward the center of the oily pool. Terrified, I sat down to stop sliding, trusting Jean to pull me out. My dress, underwear, and socks were black.

When we found a river, I took off my dress and socks, and we washed them like the Indians used to do. Jean showed me how to pound the cloth with a rock in the running stream. The dress and socks got a little cleaner, changing in color from black and oily to gray and oily, but my panties were still black. We worked hard at thinking of a good lie to cover the scare we had received. When we returned home after our adventure, we told our mothers I stumbled and sat in an oily spot in the woods. They believed the story and I escaped a hefty punishment. Avoiding, "Well-ya-damn-fool" like the plague, I hid big mishaps like this one along with the small.

I need to explain the "damn fool" reference. As a rule, Mama blamed the victim for "not caring for yourself." If I got hurt, she blamed me.

"Well, ya damn fool," she said, "if you didn't stay out in the sun so long, you wouldn't get burned." There were other admonitions: "Well, ya damn fool, if you didn't go out barefooted, you wouldn't step on a nail." One time I stepped on a nail when I had my shoes on. Undaunted, Mama said, "Well, ya damn fool, if you watched where you put your foot, you wouldn't step on a nail."

She blamed most rape victims. "Well, the damn fool shouldn't have worn a short skirt," or "Well, the damn fool shouldn't go out with people she doesn't know well." The same went for many murder victims (hanging out at a bar), house fires (frayed wiring or some other cause), and most car accidents (driving too fast or whatever) in the news.

Today I'm amazed at how confident Mama was in her judgments.

Sally has a saying, "Never in doubt but often wrong." Fits Mama perfectly.

When it was directed at me, I didn't consider the admonishment anything other than punishment. I learned not to share when I got hurt or did something wrong. I didn't want to hear "Well, ya damn fool" spoken in my mother's most scathing, punitive voice. I spared myself when I stopped revealing accidents, mistakes, and my feelings to her early on.

GALVESTON

After the war, the subject of where to live in Texas dominated my parents' conversation. Ralph Crawford – Daddy's uncle, an attorney in Galveston – said the job situation probably would be better in Galveston than in the little towns of rural East Texas, so we moved from the Piney Woods to Galveston. I was almost five.

Galveston Island is approximately 30 miles long off the coast of Texas, roughly halfway between Corpus Christi and the Louisiana border. Once the port of pirate Jean Lafitte, the city has a fabled history, full of legends of skullduggery and buried treasure. At the beginning of the twentieth century, Galveston suffered two gigantic hurricanes, in 1900 and again in 1915. Thousands of people drowned. The local government erected a seawall to protect the eastern end of the island, and required the houses to be raised several feet on stilts.

Galveston was the port where the news of the Emancipation Proclamation came to Texas for the first time. On June 19, 1865, U.S. Army General Gordon Granger brought the news that the Civil War and slavery had ended. This year, June 19 was finally declared a national holiday.

At the time of our arrival, the island was connected to the mainland by a drawbridge, to be widened during my late childhood. The first winter in Galveston I often lay with my mama on her bed on chilly afternoons, putting my bare feet between her knees for warmth, as she and I pledged our undying love and admiration for each other.

"Darlin'," I said.

"Hmm?"

"You're mighty pretty," I said.

"Thank ya."
"Darlin'…"
"Hmm?"
"You're mighty sweet."
"Thank ya."
And finally, "Darlin'…"
"Hmm?"
"You're mighty smart."
"Thank ya."
"Now you say me darlin'."

By the end of the little litany, after Mama told me I was pretty, sweet, and smart, I was asleep.

On the loss of a tooth, a fairy gave me a nickel, the cost of five candies at the store, and my favorite soft drink, Nehi Grape. Thanks to my mama and my big blue book of tales and rhymes, fairies and magic played a leading role in my early intellectual development. I loved the seven dwarfs who were so kind to Snow White; I marveled at the idea of spinning hay into gold in "Rumpelstiltskin." There were villain queens and cruel stepmothers, the big bad wolf, a giant, a wicked troll, and more. Fairy tales heralded the personal victory of good over evil every time. The tooth fairy was just one more example of the magic in my life.

I was soon introduced to hurricanes. The first of a lifetime of storms blew in from the Gulf of Mexico. Jean was spending a couple of weeks with us, and Lou Lou, her mother, back home in Talco, was frantic.

"Get my baby off that island!" she demanded.

Daddy tried to calm her, to no avail. "We are safe," he said. "We're behind the seawall."

Sure enough, the winds and rain came in a hurry. We had about twenty-four hours' warning in those days. Daddy explained the mechanics of a hurricane to Jean and me. "Hurricane winds come in a circle, first from the south, counterclockwise. Then after a time, all will be quiet as the center of the circle passes over. Then the winds will come from the other direction, but not as strong."

Jean and I sat on my parents' bed and watched the torrent outside the window. Then the wind stopped, and all was quiet. Daddy put us in the car and drove down the seawall to see what damage had been done. After about fifteen minutes we went back to the safety of the apartment. Unfortunately, we had left the window by the bed open and flooded the mattress. I didn't get into trouble because Jean did it, too.

Every Sunday, members of my family, except me of course, sang in the Crockett Place Methodist Church choir. Mama sang solos when the music called for it, her beautiful soprano filling the little building. I sat alone in the first pew under her watchful eyes. When we read the Psalm, I lagged about ten words behind everyone else. My mother was embarrassed, but the pastor insisted on waiting for me to finish. When we sang, I tried hard to understand the hymns in the *Cokesbury Hymnal*. I sang "Bringing in the Sheeps," never suspecting there was a word such as *sheaves,* and "Abide with Me." The song I had most trouble with was "Rock of Ages." I couldn't figure it out. "Rock of Ages, cleft for me, let me hide myself in thee." *Cleft*? What is *cleft*? And how can you hide in a rock? In my mind, I pictured a big rock, but I couldn't figure out how to get inside it.

Mama told me there is a God, and he loves me just as I am; nothing I do can make a difference in God's love. Hearing this, I was at first delighted, but I couldn't completely believe the part about loving me when I was bad. That was too good to be true, so I put it to the test: "What if I stole something?"

"God would still love you," Mama said.

"What if I killed somebody?"

"He would still love you."

My take-away from such conversations was I was home free with *carte blanche* approval to do anything and still be okay with God. As the years passed, I tested the Almighty many times.

My sister, Enna Frances, and I had our own rooms, but hers was infinitely more interesting than mine. As a teenager, she had various projects going, like the poster-size sheet of tin foil she designed to use as a reflector for photography. She procured the foil from the wrapping of individual sticks of gum, which meant she had to chew a lot of gum to get enough foil to put on the poster board. I helped her. It was way more interesting to hassle her than anything I had going on in my room. My interest in her stuff led to some serious conflict.

For evening entertainment, the family often played games, like "Crazy 8s" with playing cards and "42" with dominoes. I watched the play from the periphery and became good at Crazy 8s. If a friend of the family played for the first time, Daddy would let me direct the newcomer's play. I recall one time the newbie adult objected to letting a little girl decide which card to play, but Daddy was firm: let Elizabeth show you how. I didn't often lose.

Our family adopted a little homeless terrier in the neighborhood. We called him Nippy because he would lightly bite at our heels as we walked. Nippy was part of the family until the day a car hit and killed him. Daddy said it was my fault because I was supposed to watch him. I was devastated. No one told me cars sometimes hit dogs or that keeping Nippy alive was my responsibility.

Mine was an exciting world. On Christmas Eve, I lay awake trying to spot Santa Claus' sleigh in the sky outside my window. Mama and my teachers were generous with poems and songs, sprinkling them onto my days like salt and pepper on food, generating a profound love of language and its works.

The Derby

In our early years in Galveston, Jean and her parents visited us several times. They came for the University of Texas Medical Branch in Galveston because Uncle Whitey had some symptoms of a serious not-yet-diagnosed disease. Almost every afternoon at 5:00, Mama and Lou Lou took us to the beach, west of 61st Street, beyond the seawall, built to protect the city against hurricanes. We could drive on the sand, right up to the water, if we wanted. However, we didn't do it because Daddy said saltwater rusts your car. Jean and I swam in the shallow water, hunted pretty seashells, and played Beautiful Hollywood Actresses, wrapping our towels around us provocatively and posing on the hood of the car for imaginary pinups.

In the 1940s, Galveston beaches were seldom crowded, especially the ones west of the seawall, which stretched only to 61st Street. The most irritating saltwater flotsam was a scratchy seaweed riding the tide onto the shore. Otherwise, the water was clean. I discovered the saltiness of the Gulf was good for my mosquito bites. After an hour in the salt water of the Gulf, those irritated patches on my skin disappeared. While we waded in the shallow water, we might step on a crab or something else moving quickly away from our feet and tickling our toes; it didn't hurt or scare us.

Some evenings after dinner, our parents took Jean and me to a small amusement park behind the seawall on Galveston's East Beach. We rode the bumper cars, the Ferris wheel, and the roller coaster, which my mama did not approve of. The old wooden frame was creaky, and the cars careened on their path from a dizzying height to the track's end back down on solid ground.

When Uncle Joe visited us, he paid for our roller coaster tickets. I adored him.

Something unexpected happened on the merry-go-round. Called the Derby, this ride boasted a real racehorse feature. Horses and elaborate carriages, beautifully painted and decorated, were on a mechanism creating a horse race. When the ride stopped to take on new "jockeys," each winning ticket holder was awarded a free pass for another ride. Now for the weird part of the story: I could watch the horse race once or twice from the sideline and then pick the next winner on each row.

There were four horses in each row of the carousel. As they began their race to the accompaniment of a booming, earsplitting calliope, they moved forward and back, allowing one to be ahead of the others, if only for a moment. As it advanced on an unseen track, the others fell behind until another horse advanced. When the race was over, there was a winner on each row.

"How do you know which horse will win?" Mama said.

I didn't know how I knew. I guess my brain "synced" unconsciously with the device controlling the race. Jean and I would ride free many times, and when our parents made us leave our winning horses, we would give our final free tickets to two other children and point them to the next winners for a free ride.

My Untimely Murder

Connor, I need to explain how my death threats started. As I got a little older, I began to run afoul of Mama's rules of behavior. I rebelled. I rendered Mama's life more difficult, and my sister's teen years considerably more miserable than they would have been without me.

Unable to think of an appropriate way to control me, Mama defaulted to "I'll kill you if you do that again." In those days, hyperbole was my reality. Remember, my concept of *kill* came from stories about poisoned apples and the wicked queen who told a woodsman to take the pretty Snow White into the forest and cut her heart out.

To address my transgressions, Mama sometimes sent me into the yard to cut a branch off a bush with which to make stripes on my legs. I tried to find a friendly switch, one that wouldn't hurt too much. However, if I didn't get a good one, she'd pick one out, standing in the sunshine examining a thin branch of a bush, removing the leaves and making a weapon. I noticed the pink roses in her housedress had faded to almost nothing in spots. I waited for the pain and wanted to disappear along with her roses. I knew she wanted me to cry, but I refused. Instead, I stayed silently defiant.

One such time I said, "You want me to cry, but I'm not going to."

"Oh, yes you will!"

I didn't.

Mama kept her rules of behavior to herself until I broke one, and then she rushed into action. I was punished, often ignorant of what I had done wrong. One day she made me go into the pantry for punishment. When she turned to leave me there in the corner of the pantry, I stuck my tongue out at the faded roses across her back. Unfortunately, she turned and saw me.

"I'm going to kill you," she said in a hurried, harried way, and she disappeared into the kitchen. I watched her choose an old, dull bread knife about twelve inches long from the knife drawer. Upon her return to the pantry, I saw the knife and thought this time she was planning to cut my heart out, like Snow White's. Running for my life, I shot past her out the back door.

Following behind, she yelled, "You come back here! Don't run from me!"

Apparently, it was quite a show: my panicky procession gained a few neighbors chasing Mama chasing me. I counted on the neighbors to prevent my murder. Thank goodness, Melba from next door finally caught up with her and took away the weapon. We never mentioned the incident again.

In my 80-plus years of living, my feelings for my mother ranged from adoration to hatred, returning to love and compassion. When I was thirty-five, Mama said I was the most unusual child she'd ever seen. Obviously, she didn't know how to cope with me; *I* couldn't cope with me, either. Today I doubt I can be fair to her, regardless of how hard I try or how very much I want to. She was my everything when I was young: my source, my sustenance, my mentor, my security, my insecurity. I loved her even when I hated her.

Forgiveness was not a popular topic in my family. The first time I remember hearing the word *forgive*, apart from the Lord's Prayer, I was about four years old. Mama had been reading the story of Hansel and Gretel to me. I was horrified that their daddy would let their wicked stepmother take them out into the woods and leave them there.

After all their (mis)adventures, the children, loaded with the dead witch's riches, returned to their home and their father. The evil woman was dead, and their father asked if they could forgive him. They said "yes," but I said "no." I told Mama I would never have gone back home; he might do it again. *Forgiveness* didn't appear safe. At a young age, I had learned not to do foolish things; I didn't want to be a victim.

There were other examples of my unwillingness to forgive, such as the horrid queen in "Snow White," and what about Cinderella's whole stepfamily! The world was full of bad guys, and I couldn't see where my forgiveness would make it a better place to live. I resolved to hold them all responsible and make them pay, in blood if possible. And so it came to pass, as they say in the Bible, I never forgave anyone for anything.

Lately, I've been thinking about my unwillingness to forgive and forget. Throughout my long life, I've gradually learned that forgiveness is essential, and the greater the damage done to me, the greater my need to forgive. If no one hurt me, I'd have no reason to forgive. I might just go through life like a tornado, doing what I do with no reason to reflect or change course. What a disaster! It's like driving a car but never turning the steering wheel to adjust for direction and obstacles in the road. I'd run into the ditch, or worse.

I need other people. If I expect others to guide me through life, to absolve what I've done and said, I must make it transactional, *quid pro quo*, as the lawyers say. Forgiveness is a give and take, a paradox: to be forgiven, I must forgive.

THE MOTHER TONGUE

Apart from cursing, my mother used beautiful English, complete with the subjunctive "If I were..." But unlike the mothers of my friends, she had a taxonomy of swear words to use according to her degree of irritation. The first rung of her damnation ladder satisfied the perfect response to her mild irritation; "Hectoration" was the word she sometimes used for minor annoyance.

In her next circle of curses in this paradise lost were "Halifax" and "Helena, Montana." She often picked up something I had laid down—my library book, for example—and, setting it on my bed, she'd say, "I wish that was in Halifax," or the slightly louder expletive, Helena Montana, fired off with a little more volume. leading me to think it was part of a physical address. For years I thought Halifax and Helena, Montana were nicknames for hell.

Damn and *shit* were in the middle of her profanities ladder. She often said, "I'll swear and be damned!" After a while, she changed it to "I'll swear and be durned," I guess in an effort to become more spiritually appropriate. Finally, for the ultimate curse, she tossed spirituality: "Well, I'll be God damn."

In my mother's lexicon were certain phonological rules. The silent D: *Candle* was pronounced "cannel," and *handle* followed suit with "hannel." A nod to the French: *tourniquet* was "turn-a-key." My favorite of her rules involved the pronunciation of /a/ in words like *Mary* (long a), *marry* (short a). There was a huge difference in the sounds of *Gary*, a small community across the lake, and *Garry*, Mama's friend down the road. *Cary* [Cay-ry] Grant was a famous actor, not to be confused with *carry*, something you did with groceries.

Mama's words were distinct and most of her utterances grammatical. She used bad grammar for emphasis, as in, "Who don't like ice cream?" At times she played with the language. I never knew when she would lob a linguistic curve ball to me. Preparing dinner one day in my seventh year, she held aloft an evaporated milk can and recited a verse:

"Carnation Milk is the best in the land.
It comes to you in a little red and white can.
No tits to pull, no hay to pitch,
Just poke a hole in the son of a bitch."

I memorized a lot of the language I heard. I could recite from memory most nursery rhymes in the blue book and poems from school. My second-grade teacher read "The Swing," by Robert Louis Stevenson. I recall a dizzy feeling of joy over the cadence of the poem. Her voice picked up the rhythm and carried me along the swing's flight: "Up in the air I go flying again. Up in the air and down." I fell in love with language.

I memorized songs from my sister's vinyl records: Frank Sinatra, Glen Miller, and Rosemary Clooney. I could recite "Smoke That Cigarette." Remembering numbers was surprisingly easy, starting with our first phone number, 29502, in Galveston.

Uncle Ralph and Aunt Jewel

In the Galveston Yacht Basin, Uncle Ralph kept a boat, thirty-two feet long with a musty and moldy cabin for sleeping. Every Thanksgiving when duck hunting season began, he, my parents, and I spent most of the long weekend on that boat in the Intracoastal Canal just west of Galveston, "to celebrate your birthday," everybody said. Uncle Ralph and Daddy went duck hunting; Mama cooked. I got presents, a lot of mosquito bites, and more than a little attention. Each Thanksgiving Day, we marked my height on the passageway from the cabin to the sleeping quarters. I was amazed at how much higher each mark was than the year before because I couldn't remember growing.

Chugging out of the bay through the ship channel, the boat approached a drawbridge, controlled by a troll, according to Uncle Ralph. I put the big pewter horn to my mouth, trying to alert the troll to stop traffic and raise the bridge to let us pass. The horn was extremely difficult to coax a noise out of, especially a loud-enough noise to be heard from the bridge. Uncle Ralph insisted the reason I couldn't blow the horn was I wasn't holding my feet right, so as we approached the bridge, I experimented with several stances to signal the troll to raise the bridge. However, all my efforts went to nil.

Connor, at this point in my story, I should introduce you to Aunt Jewel, Uncle Ralph's wife who suffered terribly from hay fever. When we visited, she would sometimes answer the door with a white cylindrical Benzedrine inhaler hanging out of her nose. In peak allergy seasons, she used two, one for each nostril. Mama had already warned me not to question Aunt Jewel about the inhalers, so the first time I saw her with two white tusks dangling from her nose, I knew better than to laugh or tell her she looked like a walrus.

While Mama and Aunt Jewel visited with each other in her crimson bedroom, I entertained myself, sitting on the floor with a pencil and piece of typing paper or playing with one of her many cats. Mama, in her faded cotton flowers, sat across the room from Aunt Jewel. On one occasion when I was five—it must have been a good day for breathing because Aunt Jewel had no inhalers hanging—I carefully traced around the watermark on the cotton bond paper to reveal the word *Jewel*.

Dressed in a stylish green dress that hinted at her trim shape, Aunt Jewel had pulled her wiry hair straight back to resemble a gray helmet on her head or maybe a wig of steel wool.

"Look, Enna!" Aunt Jewel shouted at my mother. "Elizabeth is writing my name!" From then on, she was convinced I was brilliant.

Mama knew better, I guess, because she didn't look impressed. I tried to tell them I traced the letters, but she wouldn't listen. Maybe she couldn't see the watermark after I penciled over it.

During my childhood I came to know Aunt Jewel well. An artist, she had red flowered curtains and a red plaid bedspread in her room. When I asked Mama why Aunt Jewel didn't try to match the fabrics, the way I'd seen her do it, she said Jewel was an artist, and that explained everything. I didn't ask how because Mama would get angry with me. Sometimes she'd answer the question *why?* with, "It just does," or "Because I said so."

Although she was bossy and her voice strident with most people, Aunt Jewel was extra kind to me. I stayed with her occasionally when Mama had other business. At age five, I loved her stories about my Crawford ancestors, Scottish Protestants who left Northern Ireland in the olden days and eventually came to America as indentured servants.

"They suffered terrible hardships," she said, "working seven years to pay their passage to America so we, their descendants, could have a better, freer life. Their job was to help clear the Everglades in Florida. Imagine clearing a swamp when you've never seen a snake!" she said. I didn't know what the Everglades were, but I knew snakes. "Your ancestors organized the first sit-down strike in America and refused to work."

What's a sit-down strike? I wondered. I pictured a group of my ancestors sitting down in their red flowered living rooms. They sat on chairs, sofas, benches, stools, and the floor of my mind, with some pop-up snakes. Some had their feet up so snakes couldn't bite them.

"I wish I could thank them," I said, picturing myself approaching a group of ancestors sitting on Aunt Jewel's couch in their Sunday best, but she shook her head.

"All you can do is live a good life and try to make your Crawford ancestors proud of you. You can make their lives worth the hard times!"

From Aunt Jewel I also learned if you were kind to her cats, they would always love you. She had two dogs, one of which had no back legs; he ran all over with wheels attached to his torso.

She said, "One year for us humans is seven years for a dog. Dog years are shorter than ours."

We had lessons on flowers growing in Galveston, the Oleander City – "Oleanders are poisonous, so don't eat them," she said. I had smelled oleander leaves and never considered putting one in my mouth.

Aunt Jewel occasionally mentioned the Catholic Church, which she referred to as the "Whore of Babylon," run by an evil man called Pope. She never explained why she hated Catholics, so I didn't question her. I didn't know for sure what a whore was, and I'd never heard of Babylon. I figured I'd better just forget it because the tone of her voice made it sound like something Mama wouldn't approve of.

Today I believe the seed of Aunt Jewel's hatred of Papists, as she called them, was planted in the Catholic-Protestant wars in the United Kingdom. My Scottish ancestors were Protestants when they relocated to Ireland before they relocated to the United States early in the eighteenth century.

Huntsville, Texas

When I was eight, my sister Fran graduated from Ball High School in Galveston and wanted to study medicine. As it turned out, she didn't *want* to study anything. At the end of her first semester, she ran away with a clarinet player in the college band. But I'm getting ahead of the story.

Our parents, having little-to-no money, agreed to move to Huntsville so their first-born could go to college at Sam Houston State Teachers College. As a third grader, I failed to see the irony of attending a teacher's college to become a doctor.

Our father joined the staff in a Huntsville pharmacy, and Mama became housemother to a group of coeds. Singletary House, on a tree-lined street a couple of blocks from the college, fit romantic descriptions of 1950's boarding houses for girls: many rooms, bathrooms, a sleeping porch, and a huge dining room.

My new school in Huntsville kept the same split grade levels as Galveston. I had been November born, but instead of waiting ten months to start school in September, I began first grade in January. When we moved to Huntsville in the summer of 1947, I enrolled in the second half of the third grade, or high third. The spring semester led to low fourth in January.

Huntsville schools grouped students by some unknown-to-me criteria. I didn't know what was wrong. Parents and teachers had failed to warn me I would be in a class with smarter children; therefore, ignorant of the change, I despaired that my old ways of doing school wouldn't cut it in Huntsville. In low third grade in Galveston, I was at the top of my class without trying, but every day I sank to the bottom of my high third and low fourth classes like a rock in a Piney Woods tank. Despite all my trying to excel, I was a redheaded, freckled, pigtailed elementary school nobody, dressed in a plain homemade cotton dress and red cowgirl boots.

The rest of the class laughed at every wrong thing I did or said. I had no friends in Huntsville. Anxiety was my constant, if silent, partner. I wasn't in control of huge swaths of my life: grades, people, my own family, and even my sometimes-larcenous behavior.

The boarding house had a Coca Cola machine: five cents for a Coke. Each day, Mama emptied the nickels into a bowl on her dresser and doing so created more temptation than I could resist. I started taking a couple of nickels in the morning on my walk to school. I stopped at a convenience store before I got there and bought candy. I knew it was wrong; it was stealing. Therefore, the more nickels I took, the worse I felt about stealing, and the more I vowed to stop. However, I was locked into something I couldn't quit. The nickels I stole from Mama's dresser caused me to hate myself, and panic grew along with my loneliness and self-loathing.

My new class had poets, artists, writers, and engineers who could construct factories from tinker toys and then write a poem about them. There were mathematicians, rocket scientists, musicians, and dancers in my class. I had no talent in any of it. I felt stupid and clumsy and incredibly lonely.

The girls in the boarding house cheered me some. They let me visit their rooms and talk to them. They gave me candy. I tried to confide in them, to tell them I had to create something for my end-of-school project, but I was too scared about it to discuss it much. Then Mama forbade my visitations with the girls, insisting I wasted their time when they should be studying. Thus thwarted, I took some Milk Duds out of my secret stash and found relief in the sweet, gooey caramel.

Mama tried to teach me how to crochet a doily for the end of third grade project. She and I began the lessons simply with a chain stitch, sitting side by side at the huge table in the boarding house dining room. I learned the chain stitch fast; I was able to perform it over and over without a mistake. However, every time I tried to make different stitches required for the doily, I got a knotty mess and had to pull it out and start over. So I just crocheted a chain, a long and embarrassing chain. I pictured taking it out of the bag in front of the class, yard after yard of chainy string, and I believed I could already hear the others laugh at me.

Mama showed me many times how to crochet the doily, but I couldn't do it. My face burned hot with shame when I thought of my no-talent, nickel-stealing self. Candy offered little relief. Clutching the increasingly grubby little paper bag full of the offending chain, most nights I cried myself to sleep.

The last week of third grade arrived right after Christmas, and all I could think was that I didn't want to go to school. Monday morning, wearing a new dress Mama had made, I put on my red cowboy boots, took five nickels from the Coke money and dropped them into the pocket of my dress. Feeling completely debauched, I walked to the store where I bought Milk Duds and then went on to school. Stealing nickels had become a habit, something sweet in my morning to compensate for an increasingly black mood. My thoughts were mainly about how bad I was to steal from Mama and how stupid I was not to learn how to crochet a doily. I dreaded the semester's end when I would have to show my non-doily to the class.

Let the projects begin! Amy Jones was first with an original poem: wonderful rhythm, perfect rhyme. I hated her guts. The next person had carved a cat from a piece of wood, and then somebody showed a painting of a barn. There was also a working homemade radio. I couldn't believe it.

I did not raise my hand, and looking down, I avoided eye contact with the teacher each time she said, "Who's next?"

Each afternoon I walked home, relieved to be out of danger for a few hours, and crocheted another mile or two of chain. I was hopeless. I didn't tell my mother because I didn't know you could tell your mother about things that troubled you. I was certain I couldn't tell Mama about the nickels because she would get mad. ("Well, ya damn fool!") Mostly I quietly suffered.

Then came the last day of school. Nickels in my pockets, I couldn't even eat breakfast. In class, the remaining few students got up to show their projects, but I still didn't volunteer. I played in my head a little scenario in which I pulled miles of chain stitch out of the bag to the deafening roar of my classmates' laughter. I was dead last. Finally, the teacher called my name, and I quickly considered telling her I didn't have a project, but I was scared I'd fail low fourth grade. Smoothing some of the wrinkles in my dress with my hands, I took my soiled and crumpled bag to the front of the room.

"I wanted to learn to crochet a doily," I said, opening the bag, "but..." I reached into the bag and began feeling around for the endless chain, but something felt not quite right to my shaky fingers. From the bag, I pulled out a delicate doily about the size of my hand.

"OOOHHH," a murmur of admiration was heard. I was the most surprised person in the room. It was a crochet miracle!

Returning to Galveston

My sister ran off to get married in December, I think. In the first month after the elopement, Mama discovered me crying in my room. I said I missed Frances and didn't like being the only child in the family. It was a lie. I was really crying about myself, my loneliness, my nickel addiction, and my candy habit, but I couldn't tell her that.

My sister, age seventeen, was now a married woman, an adult. Mama cried, too. We held each other, clinging. It was the last time I remember loving my sister.

In January, we moved to a garage apartment not far from Singletary House. There were huge trees in the neighborhood, and I was just old enough at nine to enjoy climbing them. I knew my mother wouldn't like my being so high in a tree, so I didn't tell her. I could step off a tree limb onto the roof of the garage apartment, but I had to do it when she was out of the house. There was also a huge gully between my school and the apartment.

On my way home from school each day I stopped at the edge of the drainage ditch to watch children swing across and back on a rope. There was water in it only on days when it rained, so mostly children swung out over the dry concrete ditch. When I described it to her, Mama told me to stay away from there.

Never a resister of temptation, I approached the gully one day and noticed there were no children there. It hadn't rained, and the dry, gaping chasm of concrete called my name. Putting my feet on the big knot at the bottom of the rope and hanging on with both hands, I pushed off the side. As I approached the middle of my trajectory, I lost my grip and fell, landing on the cement surface below. It knocked the breath out of me, but after a couple of minutes I was able to get up and climb out of the ditch.

When I got home, I discovered a big blue and purple bruise along my left side from my hip up to my ribs. For the next few weeks, I had to take special care so my mother didn't see me undressed. I successfully hid the bruise from her as it changed from purple to blue and finally to a light green. Had she seen it, she would have first asked me what happened, and then she would have said, "Well, ya damn fool, if you had minded me, you wouldn't have gotten hurt. You could get killed doing that!" Mama usually got angry when I hurt myself. Looking back, I believe the anger masked her fear.

I passed low fourth grade. I never told my mama about the doily, and she never mentioned it. She did, however, tell me not to steal any more nickels.

At the end of school, the three of us moved from Huntsville back to Galveston, or more precisely, to Hitchcock, about ten miles north of the island. Only it was not, and never would be again, the same as before. I couldn't feel good about myself because at the end of the day, I was still just a common thief, thus unworthy of miracles. I probably owed God for the doily. Even after relocating where there were no nickels to steal, at the age of nine, I felt a black pit reserved for the worst of the damned at the center of my soul.

In the summer of my tenth year, my mother disappeared into depression, and I sank deeper into loneliness. The distance between my house and civilization could be measured in light years. In rural Galveston County, the July sun dawned early and then hung in the sky like it was painted up there.

The Depression and then WWII had set Americans back, although not to the extent of the carnage in the rest of the world. Our shortfalls were more financial and personal, the U.S. having suffered great losses of soldiers, sailors, pilots, and resources. Americans were spared the bombings and fires because we were on a different continent, and we entered the war only after

Hitler's prospects started to circle the toilet bowl. He tried to make some inroads into America by way of Mexico, but his plan was discovered by the U.S. and thwarted.

Millions of Americans had a hard time recovering from the nation's devastation. My mother had no role models to follow into the new world order. In her generation, women became housewives and mothers. Those who worked full time were usually teachers, nurses, and secretaries.

Our family of three settled into a shack in a small rural community with neither family nor friends nearby. When Mama and I were stuck at home, I think depression attacked her; she looked around and realized that life as she knew it was over.

Summertime went into slow motion. While I logged hundreds of miles on my bicycle, Mama escaped with naps. When she was awake, she was either complaining about Daddy or "teaching" me how to... how to what? Often irritable, Mama was definitely not a teacher. I tried to avoid her attention whenever I could. I read, practiced the piano, and took long walks with Sad Sack and Flea Pup through the heavy trees, shrubs, and weeds down to the bayou, about a block away. I trusted my dogs to scare away the snakes.

Fran and Carl lived in Pasadena, Texas, home of the smelliest paper mill in America, and, appropriately, I thought, Carl's putrid hometown. Mama sentenced me to a two-week term with them every June.

Fran and Carl fought a lot. In her nightgown and holding a butcher knife, she threatened to cut his throat if he touched her again; she woke me after midnight as a witness. Carl stood across the kitchen from her, still dressed in his dirty work clothes, with a bemused smile. I stood in the doorway half asleep until she said I could go back to bed.

Carl's sister was a year younger than I was, so I could hang with her some of the time. One afternoon she said we were going to memorize the Presidents of the United States in order.

"Why?" I asked.

I didn't get a satisfactory answer, but since Presidents were the activity *du jour*, I did it. Washington, Adams, Jefferson, Madison, Monroe, and so on. I considered the time a colossal waste.

A huge new secret occupied my consciousness with anxious dread: Carl groped me every chance he got. I didn't know what to do. Now I see that, had I told my parents Carl abused me and Fran pulled a knife on him in a fight, I could have avoided a miserable summer sojourn. Instead, my mother repeatedly sentenced me to those two weeks in hell, saying, "You must visit your sister because you love her so much."

SUICIDE

I remained unable to tell anyone what Fran's marriage was like, the abuse, how I hated both Carl and her, and other salient facts about my life. Some nights I cried myself to sleep, mentally putting words together to tell my parents about this horror, but during the day the words didn't come. Unforgiveness made it possible to hate my sister and her husband for terrorizing me. I would hold them both personally responsible and make them pay if I could.

My life became a perpetual effort to escape new trouble. Afraid of my father's anger and my mother's depression, I couldn't tell anyone. I practiced what to say to my mother, but I didn't have the courage. I suspected my family would implode if my parents learned of the abuse, so I pondered the situation and remained quiet. Family members mistook my silence for pouting, which my mother tried to correct by requiring me to smile. I didn't feel like smiling, and I started to flirt with ideas of suicide to escape the pressure. As I thought about killing myself, I took comfort in the notion of not having any problems afterward. I wouldn't be a thief, wouldn't get groped, wouldn't be lonely. I never thought my parents would care if I died; I felt alone in the world.

Going anywhere in the car with them was like navigating the Styx, the River of Death, what with my suicidal wish and my parents' incessant arguing over the best way to get where we were going. Before the trip, Daddy would tell us to get in the pickup. Once we were there, he would remember a couple of things he had to do before we left. In freezing cold or sweltering heat, Mama would damn him to hell several times for keeping us waiting. Out of our gate and onto the highway, my mother would say in her "damn fool" voice, "Why'd you turn right there?" Then they would argue the rest of the way to our destination. I'd sit between them trying not to hear, but her shrill voice would have cut through pea soup.

I learned to hate trips with them. And I learned to hate her. I wanted her dead. There was a day, much like any other day, when she was washing dishes and I was drying. Complaining without ceasing, she rinsed the soap off a butcher knife and set it aside for me to dry. I had some difficulty resisting an impulse to bury it in her back. I just wanted to shut her up.

Suicidal ideas held me hostage. At the same time, I suffered from acute asthma attacks brought on by allergies to just about everything in the air. I never considered the repercussions of suicide, even as I panicked through asthma. Throughout my teen years, I suffered from not being able to get enough oxygen into my lungs. Half the time I wanted to die, and the other half I was afraid I would.

After a great deal of contemplative investigation, the only way I knew to kill myself was grabbing the steering wheel and turning it into the path of an oncoming truck, unsatisfactory because I didn't want my death to hurt. The only way my death could involve a truck was throwing myself in front of a parked one. Solving the pain problem of a moving vehicle cast a shadow over the death issue. Dying, such a simple solution to my unhappiness, turned out to have a host of logistical difficulties. The devil, as they say, is in the details. I decided to sit on my hands while riding between my parents in our pickup truck and exist for the time being until I could think it through.

So, to be or not to be? These thoughts brought into focus my lack of information on the subjects of God and heaven. I knew I had a free ticket to heaven because my mama had assured me early on that God loved me; I was certain I wasn't required to *do* anything to get to heaven. But what, exactly, was heaven like? I tried to imagine myself there, but channeling all my thoughts toward St. Peter at the Pearly Gates failed to reveal a path I thought I could walk.

Death

I was forty years old before I realized my sanity from age ten was affected by chemicals. When the wind came from the north, I struggled to breathe. We didn't know what I was allergic to, but windy days and musty rooms made it worse. Several times Daddy took me late at night to the doctor's house, some fifteen miles away. I frequently contemplated dying from my illness and/or suicide because of sexual abuse.

To alleviate the asthma, my daddy brought pills home from a drug store in La Marque. Benadryl was the first, and it worked wonders for a few weeks. Then it quit working, and I was forced to take a variety of other antihistamines. I went back and forth between drugs. Benadryl made me sleepy, but I noticed I got a lot of energy from some of the others.

With regard to spiritual matters, there was no Methodist church in Hitchcock, so my parents worked with other like-mindeds and established one. We met out at a blimp base, a relic from the war some ten miles from the community. At first a pastor from a neighboring town volunteered to hold a worship service each Sunday. A year later, however, the Methodist powers that be in Texas assigned a young preacher, Perry Richardson, to minister to the little flock. I was glad to have a new consultant to answer my growing questions about life and its consequences.

Because I wasn't sure how Perry would feel about suicide, I didn't run the topic past him. Although I'd heard suicide was wrong, I also knew it was the ultimate solution to *my* problems, and I wasn't willing to relinquish it as an option. At eleven, my questions for Perry concerned more existential matters, a conjunction between real life as I knew it and belief: does a baby have a soul immediately upon conception, or is a soul appointed to a baby at the time of birth? I tried to visualize a department in heaven responsible for assigning souls to babies. I chased the issue into a mental roundhouse and finally surrendered. Surely Perry would be able to shed some light on the subject.

Wrong! He was no help. In answer to my question, Perry said, "I don't know."

One day I overheard my parents discussing missionaries, which brought them to the subject of "God's call to the ministry." Perry had discussed his call with them and specified the exact moment he knew he would be a preacher.

"When you hear God's call, you have to go!" my mother declared to my father.

What? Wait a minute! I greeted the thought with near suffocation. Her grandfather had been a Methodist minister, so I tended to believe what Mama said about churchy things.

Heretofore, I believed God's business was carried out on a voluntary basis, not you-have-to-go like the Army. What if God called *me* to be a missionary? In Africa? Yikes! I knew I couldn't go to Africa because of the snakes. I'd seen all the Tarzan movies, and every one of them had shown at least one huge snake in an African tree. I would have to avoid going there.

I suspected refusing God was bad, but life was scary enough in southeast Texas where the snakes were much smaller and on the ground, not waiting in a tree to jump on you. At night I added to my prayers a sincere request to God not to call me to be a missionary anywhere in the world because everywhere had snakes.

Except Ireland. I recalled one lesson on ancestors when Aunt Jewel told me St. Patrick banished snakes from Ireland. However, I suspected I couldn't be a missionary in Ireland because I'd not heard that Ireland needed Christian help from America. Horrible though our Texas snakes were, I could identify them and felt reasonably hopeful I could continue to avoid them.

Besides, I preferred a call to be a movie star or airline stewardess.

Hitchcock, Texas

In our early Hitchcock days, Aunt Lou Lou, recently widowed, and Jean came to stay a few months with us. I was ten, Jean thirteen. Mama and Daddy were thirty-nine, and Lou Lou thirty-three. We were crowded but comfortable.

Daddy was busy building a living room onto our Quonset hut, having just finished the two bedrooms. For a short time, Jean and I attended the same school, classes I liked a lot because I was once again able to do well without much work. Hitchcock schools had no high-low plan, so the superintendent of the tiny district first decided I would go into fourth, half of which I had already done in Huntsville. Or as I have already explained, low fourth had really been done to me.

The plan for me to attend the low fourth grade a second time, however, was problematic because I had already been exposed to long division, a strange new disease from another planet. Each time this fourth grade teacher gave us "short division" problems, I told the class short division wasn't useful and not worth learning. "So here's how to do *long* division."

Connor, I didn't know any more about long division than Homer's goat. Moreover, because I was so disruptive in fourth grade, the superintendent and Mama decided I should skip fourth and go on into fifth grade. A stellar plan. Although I missed out on the multiplication tables and long division, I could do the other subjects just fine.

In fifth grade, I exploded. I became rebellious in school, interrupting lessons, openly defying teachers, and distracting other students. I took my various morning allergy pills and broke most of the classroom rules. Some days I was sent to the superintendent's office. If the school had asked my mother to help control my behavior, she would have killed me and then made me act right. However, I guess my parents didn't know how much power they had.

In fifth grade, I met a friend who would come through life with me. Beautiful beyond imagination, Jane was also quick to laugh and have fun. I was a terrible influence on her because she fell into my misbehavior as though she'd been born for it. I could always get Jane to laugh. My favorite ploy was to make a fart noise with my hands and watch her crumple up with laughter. I continued through high school doing things that got her into trouble with the teacher. I made faces at her when the teacher wasn't looking. She'd laugh. I poked her with the sharp point of a compass. She'd jump up cursing, which made *me* laugh.

Jane's hair was long, brown, and very shiny, and when I learned how she kept it pretty, brushing it 100 times each night, I did the same with mine. However, that was about as far as I could go to be like her. She had a knockout smile, showing her white, Chiclets teeth.

Mine was a loving jealousy. I've never had any kind of bad feelings for her. Jane's mother made beautiful dresses, all in the same pattern, but the brilliant colors and silky nylon fabrics enhanced Jane's beauty. My mother made my dresses out of feed sacks. Colorful they might have been, but the fabric was rough and scratchy. I felt plain and dowdy. I repeatedly asked for colorful, silky nylon dresses like Jane's, but Mama said, "No."

I remember thinking, *If I ever have a little girl, I will not tell her no*. Maybe if Mama had reminded me we had no money, I would have understood. Maybe it would have been easier to go without, but probably it wouldn't. I was not into thinking of others.

When Kiss was born in 1965, I was able to fulfill my promise of not telling her no. I spoiled her shamelessly.

Cousin Jean

During the year after Jean's father's death, she and I were inseparable, not because we wanted to be, but because we were out in the country, and she was stuck with me. I made her life miserable. First, although she was three years older, I was taller; therefore, our fights usually ended with me the victor: Jean cursed at me, and I threw rocks at her. At times she got so angry she could hardly speak. She'd cry and go inside to complain to our mothers. After a short time, we would apologize at Lou Lou's insistence and go play again.

Blonde and blue-eyed, slight of frame, Jean was prettier. She could wear boys' tees and dress shirts and look so put-together, as our mothers described her. When I tried on boy's shirts, they didn't fit. The tees pulled the fabric tight over my chest, revealing way too much of me underneath, and the shirts wouldn't button down the front. Even a larger size caused what Lou Lou called "gaposis." Of course, I hated wearing my little girl dresses made of rough feed sack material. I wanted a new look, a different look, anything not resembling *me*.

Jean was also smarter, and I was jealous of her. An ace in mathematics, she brought home stellar report cards, and she was more focused. All our creative activities came out of Jean's brain, mine being distracted most of the time.

In Galveston, Jean was by far the most accomplished cousin our extended family had seen. She and Aunt Jewel's daughter, Lally Ann, entertained themselves with solving math problems in their various high school texts. Thinking them weird, I wanted no part of it. In her twenties, Lally joined the mathematics faculty at the University of Houston after she completed her Ph.D.

The differences between Jean and me were obvious to our parents. While Jean was brilliant with anything mathematical, she couldn't spell a lot of words her brainpower required. It was not uncommon for her to interrupt my homework sessions with spelling requests for her own writing. When I graduated from UT, she sent a card misspelling her sentiments: *Congradulations!*

Unlike Jean, I was a "story" girl. By age six I had memorized almost all of the nursery rhymes in my huge blue book. At ten I devoured my late grandfather's copy of Edith Hamilton's *Gods and Heroes*. The adults in the family were impressed, but I didn't think it anything noteworthy. I was interested in stories. The only books we had in the house were my grandfather's complete set of Dickens, some classical myths and legends, and something called *The Vicar of Wakefield*, which I found either too boring or too difficult to wade through.

When adults praised me, it was usually for my voracious appetite for Story. Seldom seeing anything remarkable or even good about myself, I discounted their accolades for three reasons:

- I didn't know the multiplication tables;
- I couldn't add a column of figures and get the same number twice;
- There's nothing unique about liking stories.

After graduation from Ball High School in Galveston, Jean attended the University of Texas, married a psychiatrist along the way and, in the 1960s, finished her education with a Ph.D. in psychology from Columbia University at age twenty-nine. She joined the faculty at Columbia and stayed more than fifty years to become professor emerita.

One day in Phoenix in the early 2000s, I read a *New Yorker* article about the *Diagnostic and Statistical Manual* (DSM)—the taxonomy of mental disorders, the standard in the insurance industry. Before the DSM, insurance claims were vague and, in my own medical terminology, all over the place. I'm sure there were other facets of the DSM, but the only one I remember is about insurance. Imagine my surprise to find Jean's comments in and contributions to the article! I realized for the first time how famous she was. I was aware she had made countless trips to Italy as a consultant. She had focused on PMS and a couple of other issues in her own research. I knew she designed statistical studies for some medical corporations, but I hadn't put it all together until I read the article. She was one of the original writers of the first DSM.

In her eighties Jean got Covid-19, the dreaded virus at the outbreak of the pandemic. She didn't die, but the infection led to something called Long Covid, which incapacitated her almost completely, causing brain fog and dementia. What a tragedy.

The Pig

One early Friday morning after Jean and Lou Lou moved to Galveston, Daddy went to the feed store and brought home a baby pig. He put it in the chicken house and told Mama it cost fifteen dollars, a capital investment in the early 1950s.

On that fateful day, Mama and Frances were on the screened back porch drinking coffee. Fran wore a maternity top that could not possibly conceal her eighth month of pregnancy and baggy pants pulled tight across her huge belly. Mama wore what she always wore – a cotton dress, plain except for a tiny fade of flowers. Having made several such dresses for herself without collar or other ornament, she always looked the same, no makeup, faded cotton dress, and worn, low-heeled shoes.

"The pig is in the chicken house. I'll build a sty when I get home this afternoon," Daddy said, and left for work.

I was in my bed on the other side of the wall from the porch, pretending to be asleep but really eavesdropping. Frances had left Carl a second time in the ten months they'd been married. She was complaining to Mama about how bad he was. I hoped I could glean some information from the discussion to help me cope with Carl's abuse.

As Daddy's black Ford pickup truck disappeared in a cloud of crushed oyster-shell dust down the country road, all three of us heard the pig under the house. *"Grrn! Grrn! Grrn!"* I jumped out of bed and ran to the back porch in time to see the pig disappear into the hot whiteout kicked up by the truck still suspended over the road.

"Well, shit!" Mama said, uttering something about the fifteen dollars as she scurried out the screen door after the pig. A few minutes later, she returned through the oyster-dust cloud, the squirming pinky in her arms, and put it back in the chicken house. Then she hammered a nail in the door to hold it closed and returned to the back porch, out of breath. Before she could sit down, however, we heard the pig again, first under the porch where we sat, and then in the clear, heading for the driveway and the wider world down the white dusty road.

"*Grrn! Grrn! Grrn!*" This time the piglet ran as fast as his short little legs would carry him. He made it to the driveway and out on the road. Mama grabbed her car keys and fairly ran to the car, her faded roses blowing up behind her. On the way, the Fury produced another oyster shell cloud down the road.

A few minutes later, Mama returned through the settling haze with the pig inside the car. When she got out and retrieved the pig, she hiked her housedress up to swaddle it. By this time Mama was screaming at the pig and cursing my father. After securing the chicken house door closed extra tight with three nails, she returned to the back porch.

Pigs, even baby pigs, run fast. I could hardly believe it: a third time, breaking out of the henhouse, the little pig grabbed freedom by the throat and sprinted past the porch. This time, however, he avoided the road and went under the barbed-wire fence to the neighbor's farm where there was a huge pigpen in the back pasture. It probably smelled like home to him. He squealed for his life while he tried to knock on the door to get into the neighbor's pigsty.

"Well, I'll be God damn!" Mama said, banging her coffee cup down in a splash on the table and set out for the pig again. About fifty yards away from the neighbor's sty, the little pig squealed his alarm, and the resident sow, thinking one of her babies was loose and in trouble, bawled her panic. She made a terrible racket, something like a loud moaning growl, trying to get out to him. This was the scene awaiting my mother and sister.

"Frances," Mama yelled, "come help me carry this pig. Elizabeth, get the big wooden box out of the garage. Bring me the hammer and some nails and a board. I'm going to put him in there."

My pregnant sister and my portly mother hustled around to a break in the fence and ran for the pigsty behind the neighbor's barn. As Mama grabbed the front feet and Frances got the back, the little pig screamed; then the sow screamed and started jumping and biting the top board off the sty. Then Mama screamed, and both she and Frances ran with the pig straight to the barbed-wire fence, where they stopped in a huge ant bed. As I exited the garage – wooden box, boards, hammer, and nails in hand – I saw my mother, my sister, and the pig. Everyone was screaming now: the sow, Mama, Frances, and the little pig, whose front legs were racing double-time, working Mama's arms up and down, right and left; the back legs were jerking Fran's arms.

While both Mama and Frances did an Irish clog dance with their feet to get the ants off, I placed the open end of the box below the bottom barbed wire of the fence. Pushing the pig under the fence and into the box, Mama's look said if I let this pig get away from me, she would kill me. The porcine Houdini stuck his little pink nose out of the box, and I hit it with the hammer as hard as I could. His noise and fight increased despite the hammer blows on his head. I hit the baby pig a couple more times right between his eyes as hard as I could before Mama got to us, but the blows I landed on his head did nothing to slow him down. He still screamed and jumped around inside the big box, sticking his nose out between the boards I was nailing across the top.

Mama ran faster than I'd ever seen her move to where I waited with the box of pig on our side of the fence. She secured the boards to the top and then put the box in the garage. Closing the door, she was certain he could not escape again. And he didn't.

The Little Farm

In Hitchcock, I noticed for the first time how easily Daddy could assume a worker identity. At work as a welder, he wore khaki shirts with holes burned into the sleeves from the torch. As a pharmacist, he wore a white tunic with a button Mandarin collar. He looked like a barber. At home, he used new welder words, like *drag up*, meaning to leave a job. His speech and clothes reflected his role. As a carpenter, building us a house, he wore a canvas belt to hold his hammers and other tools. I learned a new vocabulary of carpenter words: plane, square, level, plum, ball peen hammer, solenoid switch and many others.

In drugstores where Daddy worked, I examined cosmetics and over-the-counter pills and potions. My mother used O.J.'s Beauty Lotion and Pond's Cold Cream. And to cure bodily complaints, there were Carter's Little Liver Pills and Lydia Pinkham's whatever-that-was. Early on, I learned what suppositories, antihistamines, and Merthiolate did. Mercurochrome, Merthiolate, and gentian violet killed germs. The adults around me talked a lot, and I soaked it all in.

From Mama I learned cooking and sewing words like *sear* and *placket*, words we seldom hear today. My parents never dumbed down their vocabularies for me. I usually learned the words by considering them in the context of their use, since I didn't ask any questions. "Sear the roast before you put it in the oven to get the brown appearance," she said, or "The placket goes on the left side," placing a safety pin to hold the two sides where the zipper should go. Lou Lou said Mama didn't finish the clothes she made for me and relied on safety pins to hold them together. It was true, but it wasn't the reason I didn't like them.

On Uncle Ralph's boat, Daddy used boat language, not a phony shiver-me-timbers language, but real vocabulary, like *galley*, meaning kitchen; *head*, meaning toilet; and *foc'sle*, meaning something I couldn't quite figure out. It could have been the sleeping part of the cabin, or the engine part. My father didn't suffer children, to use Jesus' words; he was usually out of sorts with me. If I asked him a question, he'd say, "Go away, little girl. You bother me." Then he'd laugh, but I knew I'd better go to another room. I think he got the joke from W. C. Fields, whom he often quoted. "Scram," he said if I didn't go fast enough.

Daddy's favorite W.C. Fields joke was about a teetotaler trying to get Fields to stay sober. She put a worm into a glass of water, where it swam around happily. Then she put the worm into a glass of alcohol. The worm curled up and died. She said to Fields, "What does this prove?"

He said, "It proves if you drink enough alcohol, you won't be bothered with worms."

On our six acres, Daddy planted a big garden. He taught eleven-year-old me to drive the tractor. He built the chicken house and bought precious yellow baby chicks, which Jean and I braved the cold and wet of February to admire and play with. Daddy made a shelter for them with a light bulb over their heads to provide warmth.

***

On the farm in the 1950s, Daddy showed Jean and me how to make kites out of newspaper and fly them across the road where there were no trees, putting them in the air early in the morning before it got too hot and staking them by tying the string to a barbed-wire fence. He taught us to light a good fire for cooking. He planted popcorn for us in the garden. On summer days, we could hear the corn pop in the field.

Between fights with each other, Jean and I read our books or flew our kites, leaving them up when we went home for lunch.

Some days we cooked our own food, digging a hole in the back yard and burying a coffee can, meat, potatoes, and carrots inside, under a campfire.

As a parent, my father was something of a "trainer." During educational psychology courses at the University of Texas, I came to understand that his teaching style agreed with B. F. Skinner's operant conditioning theory—comparing the brain and its mysteries to a black box where stimuli are produced for desired results. To illustrate the theory, the Russian scientist, Pavlov, rang a bell near a dog and then put food in front of him. Before long, the dog salivated when he heard the bell, no food in sight.

Put something into the box, the theory goes, and the desired result comes out, no need to investigate how it happens or even how the box works to bring forth the learning. Slap Elizabeth hard in the face when she vomits the castor oil (the stimulus), and she will not throw up again (the desired result).

Daddy's training methods for our bird dog puppies was painful to watch. He attached a rope to Sad Sack and Flea Pup's necks and when they wandered away, he jerked the rope hard. The puppies were airborne before they landed with a yelp and a thud back at his feet. I tried to intercede for them, but he sent me away. Each time he left, I stroked the puppies and crooned to them to try to make up for their harsh training. He later gave up training bird dogs because he said I ruined them. I've always suspected Mama made him stop.

One dark night my parents and I were in the pickup truck going home from a pharmacy in another town when Daddy suddenly slammed the brake as hard as he could. Seated between my parents on the front seat, I panicked as we skidded forward. Then I saw in the light of an oncoming car an outline of something in our lane. In an instant, Daddy saw there was a car in the other lane coming toward us and a car in front of us, stopped, lights off. He saw a culvert and ditch on our right. In the second before impact, I screamed. Daddy turned sideways, almost facing me on the bench seat, slapped my face hard and yelled at me to shut up (the stimulus). That's when we crashed into the other car.

The oncoming car stopped when we hit the dark car. Standing on the side of the road, listening to my father berate the driver of the other car, I quietly chewed my plastic wallet into little pieces.

"Look what you done to my car!" the other man said.

"Your car!" my furious father bellowed. "Why, you stupid sombitch..."

I was not privy to the rest of this discourse. Mama shepherded me back into the pickup; the drivers exchanged phone numbers, and I never heard any more about it.

I don't have to wonder whether the black box between my ears made the right associations between stimulus and response: I stopped vomiting at four and screaming at ten.

After two bedrooms, my father created yet another expansion of our Quonset hut, which had begun to resemble a real house. He was indefatigable and resourceful. Until recently I never realized how hard he worked to make a home for my mother. I accepted the constant hammering, sawing, and sanding in the spirit of an American teenager; I wasn't aware of it most of the time. I don't understand how I didn't notice the almost constant noise of building and didn't credit my father for all his hard work, but I didn't. "How sharper than a serpent's tooth to have a thankless child." I wish I could show him today I am finally aware of how hard he worked to build a life for Mama and me.

Daddy was ever alert to any slip in my grades. My only failing grade came in sixth-grade geography. Mama was livid. I explained the red D, insisting geography was so boring it didn't deserve studying. I could see no value in it.

"They teach what crops grow in Africa, how much rain falls in the desert, and other stuff I don't care about," I said.

"You will begin to care right now and get in there and read a chapter. I'll ask questions to see how well you've learned the lesson," she said. "Bring it up to an acceptable grade, or I'll tell your father." All I needed to motivate me to study geography.

Another thing, I had no idea how to wear homespun dresses with pride, as Aunt Lou Lou suggested when I complained to her. I had no pride. When she suggested that I "be myself," I didn't want to. Myself was totally unacceptable to me. I hated being me with my crazy curly auburn hair, ugly shoes, rough farm clothes, and growing breasts. I wanted to be, needed to be, someone else, anyone else.

A Baffling Life

After a few weeks, Aunt Lou Lou and Jean moved to Galveston, into an apartment in one of the old Victorian houses just off Broadway: high ceilings in their three large rooms, beautifully ornate mahogany woodwork, and no closets. I often asked if I could go home with them, and all agreed.

Mother and daughter were readers. Lou Lou loved women's magazines and bought them every month at the checkout counter of the grocery store. Jean sat on the floor and read all the stories in the magazines, then bragged to me about it. Cross-legged, she looked good in her pretty clothes, wearing pretty glasses to correct her myopia. I wanted to be, not like her, but I wanted to be her.

At nine, I became a reader, too, but early on, reading was a chore for me. There were no children's or young-adult books out in the boonies. The first book I could read came from my late grandfather's library: Edith Hamilton's *Gods and Heroes*. At nine, I couldn't pronounce most of the names, but the stories were interesting. Although it was not about a Greek, the best story was about Scheherazade, which I read as "Ske-za-rady." She was one of the wives of the ruler who created stories to stay alive by entertaining her cruel master. As long as he was interested in her stories, he didn't kill her.

Ever a critic, I thought Latin and Greek gods and goddesses were a bit unappealing with their convoluted plots and confusing, un-heroic personalities. Their names were easier than Scheherazade's, but I still botched some. Persephone was "Percyphone," as I recall.

There were also various volumes of an incomplete set of encyclopedias, which I read and tried to understand. Fascinated by planets, I read and re-read entries about Earth, Mars, and the rest. In the mid-1950s, information about the solar system was sparse, rendering the content about outer space very easy to read and remember.

When I stayed weekends in Galveston with Lou Lou and Jean, we made a late-night trip to a newsstand down on Post Office Street, the Interurban Queen, not far from the infamous red-light district. For me, Galveston held many mysteries, such as the rumored open sex trade, the business of mariners who had been at sea a long time.

Lou Lou was calm and quiet in the midst of chaos. I didn't have to keep my guard up against her. I tried to reveal my unhappiness to Jean and her, but when I told them I was depressed, Lou Lou said, "Don't feel that way." She said it wasn't polite to bring down a happy mood among others. I grew up knowing the way I felt was wrong, but not knowing how to fix it.

As time passed and my years in school increased, summers were still and endless. Mama insisted I go to Pasadena to spend a couple of weeks with Fran and Carl. I begged her not to make me go, but she was adamant.

In Pasadena, each day Carl called home at least once. Fran's voice let everyone hearing her know she didn't like him and hated talking to him on the phone. "Hello," she said in her most expressive Eeyore tone. All Carl's questions were answered in a well-you-damn-fool voice although she didn't say the words: "(Well-you-damn-fool,) I'm cooking dinner," or "(Well-you-damn-fool,) I'm busy!"

During my middle school years, I discovered inhaling the acetone in nail polish remover led me into a numb, dreamy state. So I did, reprising my old standby character defect of stealing as often as possible. I began to sneak nail polish remover into my purse when I had a chance, while either waiting for Daddy to get off work at the drugstore or on a shopping trip with Mama. I craved a dizzy disconnect from reality.

There was a new neighbor down the road, a beautiful young woman named Jan who had an older husband. I visited with her while her husband was at work. We played Beauty Shop, brushing and combing our hair and applying lipstick to our mouths in varying shades. One of those days she invited me to spend the night on her couch so we could play again the next day. During the night, her husband knelt by the couch, his hand in my pants, crooning how we could be very special friends. Still pretending to be asleep, I turned over. He went into the kitchen but came out again. I told him to stop and leave me alone. Then I ran into the bedroom and told Jan what he did. Her reaction was to ask me not to tell anyone. If I did tell, she would tell my parents I was stealing nail polish remover.

A few days later, Lou Lou got suspicious because she smelled the polish remover when I got close to her. She told my mother, and together they told me those fumes could cause brain damage. I stopped huffing polish remover and unhappily resigned myself to feel what I had tried so hard to escape.

Mama and Lou Lou were ever conscious of impending doom. One day Jane and I were discussing going on a bus to a movie in Galveston. Mama said, "Okay, but don't take any candy from a strange man."

"Mama, why would a strange man offer us candy?"

"White slavery," Lou Lou said. Jane and I must have looked confused, but she continued, "They'll kidnap you and make you their slave."

"Oh," we said.

Later, on the bus, Jane and I discussed the concept of white slavery. My only knowledge of any kind of slavery was like Mammy in *Gone with the Wind*. I tried to picture myself cleaning a huge house with a red bandana on my head. It didn't scare me, but I felt sure I would never accept candy from a strange man, just to be sure.

Frances and Carl continued their lifestyle of war and peace. She would leave him in Pasadena and bring her baby to stay with us in Hitchcock. Then she would go back to Pasadena, have another baby and leave, bringing us two babies, Wayne and Jerry. A couple of times, Carl threatened to do something to me. In times of separation, he would come to our house contrite, promising never to do it again, and talk Fran into going back. Daddy put a loaded gun under the cushion of his chair so he could easily get it while Carl was in the house.

Fran was also a victim, but I couldn't see it. I thought she was complicit in Carl's guilt. I have seldom given her credit for the good she was able to do for herself and her children. When Wayne was a baby, she went back to nursing school and became an RN. Then she worked at Harris Hospital in the premature nursery for several years. She studied for a bachelor's and a master's in nursing and graduated. She succeeded at the hard, demanding days of being a single mother with three children. I hated Carl, and I hated her, too, for bringing him into the family. Most of my young life, I blamed her for just about every wrong thing in my life.

New Friends

In sixth grade, Sally came to the little country school. While I had a terrible influence on Jane, Sally had a good influence on me. Her behavior in class was exemplary, and she was smart. More than anyone else, she showed me a better way to live, and although I couldn't always do it, at least I had another model in my repertoire when acting out failed me. Today Sally remains a friend who makes me want to be a better person.

I couldn't believe it! Sally read the newspaper. On our sleepovers, when we arrived a couple of hours before her parents came home, she spread the *Houston Chronicle* on the floor in the living room and read every boring page of it.

Three sets of parents—Jane's, Sally's, and mine—transferred us to a neighboring school district in September of eighth grade. Leaving Hitchcock behind, the three of us enrolled as transfer students in La Marque Independent School District. I remember Mama warning me that misbehavior in the new school would return me to Hitchcock. She said she'd kill me.

In eighth grade, I enjoyed Sally and Jane as steadfast friends; Jo Ann, a classmate who lived not far from the school, adopted us. Jo Ann had brown hair and brown eyes with an orange birthmark covering a small bit of the brown in her right cornea. She wore the same style to school every day: white shirt, dark gabardine skirt, and a leather jacket. Her skin was flawless.

Jo Ann was headstrong. She knew exactly who she was and what she liked and disliked. She decided mid-eighth grade to stop biting her fingernails. I didn't know there were people with self-control. My fingers were often in my mouth, and despite being harassed by my parents, I could not stop tearing at my nails and cuticles with my teeth.

"I don't like school," Jo Ann said, "and I can't wait to get out!" A quick review of my attitude toward school led me to agree with her and the not-liking part. However, not going to college scared me. What on earth would I do instead? What would my father say? My parents just had a learner's permit with Enna Frances, but with me, they acted like they had the authority to propel me anywhere they wanted me to go. College was not a question of "if" but "where." They took no chances of letting me decide this part of my future.

Around this time, we got our first television set. When I got home from school, Mama and I turned to Popeye cartoons for entertainment. We'd eat a snack and laugh at Olive Oyl. Tall and skinny, hair in a low bun at the back of her head, Olive was the beauty of both sailors' affections. One of the themes of Popeye, of course, was the power of eating spinach.

For us the main attraction was the competition between Olive's two would-be suitors. Mama and I laughed until the tears came over the sailor man's eyes popping out of his head at the sight of the beautiful Olive, who was, of course, unusually unbeautiful. Bluto would attack Popeye, who miraculously manifested a can of spinach and opened it by turning his pipe into a can opener. Then his forearm muscles did what his eyes had done. With his newly acquired strength, he knocked Bluto out of the picture and Olive swooned and sighed, "Oh, Popeye!" The plot stayed the same each day, but it still made us laugh; we never tired of it.

Television in the early days was black and white, and there was only one channel in Houston. Each evening after dinner the three of us would watch a couple of programs. Sometimes during the day, Channel 2 ran only a test pattern until something else came on. Fairly quickly, writers and producers provided new entertainment. An early huge success was Lucille Ball's show, "I Love Lucy." Almost all of television news, talk shows, and some dramas were live, meaning they were coming to us in real time. Popeye, however, and other cartoons were on film.

High School

Together Connie and I decided we could speak French; all we had to do was leave off the last sound of every word. In "Fren," *school* became "schoo," *biology* was "bioloj," and *English* "Engli." She and I became quite adept at this new language, but everyone in earshot thought we were nuts.

Jo Ann and Sally wielded the most influence on me in the matter of grooming. Both friends insisted I polish my saddle oxfords when they looked dirty. Jo Ann proved plain clothes could look elegant and "put together," but I could never get there. Jane and her mother taught me the rule about brushing my teeth before bed. Connie and Sally's insistence on finishing my homework and my parents' demand for good grades kept me out of trouble. I maintained good, but not great, levels of achievement, just enough to stay okay with my parents.

Ninth grade at the new school, La Marque High School, is something of a blur. Jane, Sally, and I each found a way into the same social group on differing paths. The popular students took one look at Jane, and her status was accepted for life. Jane added good manners and a happy disposition to her drop-dead beauty. Gregarious Sally made friends easily and so comfortably fit into the social fabric of the new school. I steered my personality away from troublemaker toward clown. I would do anything for a laugh.

My grandfather's books were all I had out in the country, but in ninth grade, I found the La Marque High School library. I discovered Anya Seton's historical novels, Frank Yerby, whose romances featured one woman and two men, and others. The librarian, Miss White, was not among my admirers. I'm sure she thought I was impudent and insulting because I was. One day she called my mother.

"Mrs. Crawford, I called to let you know Elizabeth checked *Forever Amber* out of our library," she said.

"Did she not turn it back in?" Mama said.

"No, no, I'm calling because I just wanted to let you know some people consider it to be inappropriate for a young girl," the librarian said.

"If it's not appropriate, what's it doing in your library? Elizabeth has my permission to read anything in the high school library."

Thus began a life of reading to escape reality. My behavior in school did a 180 – well, maybe a 90.

Jo Ann forbade me to see a girl named Kay because she had a bad reputation. I guess I didn't have much discernment where people were concerned, so I thought Jo Ann was being too critical of Kay. Then I went to Galveston with Kay and her family. Her parents let us out of the car to walk on the seawall while they went to take care of some business. Boys driving by would whistle when they passed us, making me very uncomfortable.

A car stopped by us on our walk and invited us to go with them. To my horror, Kay agreed and opened the back door and got inside their car. I was left to choose whether to go with Kay or stay on the seawall by myself with no way to get back home to Hitchcock. I got into the car, terrified. I felt more alone than ever before. I didn't agree with Kay that going off with people you don't know is safe, and I knew I couldn't tell anyone about this. If my parents found out, they'd kill me. At Jo Ann's insistence, I was no longer Kay's friend.

Jo Ann didn't smoke or drink; she was also bossy about us doing it. Never unsure about anything, she had a rigid code of conduct. For example, she didn't like my improvised earrings; I had put safety pins through my pierced earlobes. I didn't know how to think about things, so I adopted her perceptions when I could. By our senior year, Connie, Sally, Jane, and I were kind of scared of Jo Ann and what she thought of us.

Travels

It was 1954. Welding jobs became scarce in Texas City, so my father went to Pasco, Washington, to work. The plan was, when school was out for the summer, Mama and I would join him in the Great Northwest. It was a summer of travel for us. I had completed the ninth grade.

On our weekends in Washington, Mama, Daddy, and I explored the whole state. Growing up in Galveston hadn't prepared me for snowy White Pass near Mt. Rainier. I had never seen so much white, piled high by snowplow at the side of the highway.

On the banks of the Columbia River, we watched Native Americans fish with nets for salmon swimming and jumping waterfalls, returning to the place where they were spawned. This was a strange new world. We also ate our fill of cherries and other fresh fruit in Walla Walla.

On a call to Uncle Ralph and Aunt Jewel, Daddy learned their son Charles Ralph was in Portland, Oregon. Charles was considerably older than I, maybe ten years or more. He joined the Navy right out of high school and served on a minesweeper during the war in Korea. Although I was not around him much in his high school years, I knew him as a smiling Tom-Sawyer type, a congenial teenager who wore his baseball cap backwards. Mama told me when he was young, he occasionally walked like a monkey, holding his mother's hand as they walked down the streets of Galveston. He let his arm hang limp and walked with an irregular gait until Aunt Jewel noticed what he was doing and made him quit.

I don't remember how we located him in the crowds around the ships, but we found him and made our way to the Portland

Zoo, where the rain and steamed windows hid the beautiful setting. The four of us sat in the car where the adults excitedly chatted about the miracle of finding each other on the Portland waterfront and Mama began to serve our lunch.

Mama's meals often lacked coherence. For our picnic at the zoo, she loaded her wonderful Southern fried chicken and potato salad on to paper plates, and for dessert, delicious Walla Walla cherries. To drink she put bright red tomato juice in three glasses. We only had three. Finding an empty Kleenex box on the floor in the back seat, Mama propped the third glass on the seat between us and put the flimsy carton next to it for support.

We talked and laughed with Charles about things we had seen in Washington, and somewhere in the middle of our conversation, I picked up the empty Kleenex box and put it on the floor, not realizing the juice would spill. We were parked on an angle, Mama on the downhill side of the car. The tomato juice looked like a red moat around her butt. Horrified, I knew I would have to tell her what I had done because she, busy talking and laughing with Charles, hadn't discovered it herself.

I began in a whisper, "Mama, I spilled the tomato juice."

After I said it a few times, she turned to me and said, "What!"

"I spilled the tomato juice."

Looking down at the car seat soaking up the red juice, she sputtered a moment and then let out a cry of agony. "Well, I'll be God damn!"

I feared for my life.

The next few minutes were hell. I was so sorry I'd caused the spill, but what made it even worse, the juice ran downhill and so missed me altogether. I wished the red menace had soaked me and not Mama. Daddy continued to face the front of the car. Charles, with a huge smile Mama couldn't see, made eye contact with me a couple of times. The atmosphere inside and the rain outside the car sparked electricity.

Daddy said, "I think I'll go look at the bears."

Charles said, "Me, too."

When I said I, too, wanted to see the bears, Mama said, "Oh hell no! If I can't go look at the bears, neither can you!"

Daddy and Charles abandoned me in our 1953 Ford to suffer my mother's vocal anger alone.

Connie and Sally

In tenth grade, my close friends and I proceeded as though I had not been gone three months. One sunny afternoon Sally and I were musing about hairstyles we found in *Seventeen Magazine*, or more precisely, we discussed my lack in the style department. Sally said I would look good with an Italian boy haircut. Having never seen an Italian boy didn't enter my decision to go with it. I was desperate for anything to potentially improve me. She cut off my long hair, unprepared for the curl which seized each strand, and forced it into a different direction from all the others. To use Daddy's description, my hair looked like "a stump full of granddaddy spiders."

About twice a year, Sally, Jo Ann, Patsy, and I were invited to spend the weekend at the home of Connie's Aunt Titter and Aunt Thelma. I'm not sure exactly how they were related to Connie, but they were very dear. Thelma was the widow of a Navy war hero, I think, and perhaps Titter [a nickname] was his sister. They had a Spanish colonial home on Galveston's west end, close to the beach. We girls visited with the aunties, walked to the beach, and spent lots of time just talking and telling stories. Connie's stories were the best! Like the one about the fireman being thrown off the speeding fire truck in front of their house. Aunt Titter ran out to the street with a pillow to put under his head. Connie had loads of stories about her family, and I did, too. I don't remember any funny stories about Jo Ann's and Sally's relatives.

Connie's mother and grandmother played a significant role in my growing up. I loved being around them because they would sit and talk to us girls about anything. About everything!

Connie's mother, Lydia, was wonderful. She kind of adopted our small circle of friends and considered us without fault in every situation. No matter what scrape I got myself into, Lydia would insist I was not guilty. I loved her; she was so different from my own mother who blamed me when things went awry. I am not saying it *wasn't* my fault; it was just such a relief to be with an adult who believed in me.

In the summer before eleventh grade, given the failure of the tenth-grade haircut to make me happy with my appearance, Sally and I put our heads together and sought another way to end, once and for all, my dissatisfaction with how I looked. Sally said I should become a blonde.

"I read how to do it," she said. We were sitting on her bed perusing a *Seventeen*. "You just mix ammonia and peroxide and put it on the hair."

She jumped up and I followed. In the bathroom she found a bottle of hydrogen peroxide, but the ammonia was a little harder to locate. She finally found it in the kitchen under the sink, a warning lost to us.

I watched her measure the concoction: two parts ammonia to one part peroxide. The fumes were terrible, but they were nothing in the bottle compared to on my head! I had to go outside to breathe. I don't remember how I was able to endure this torture, but it wasn't a long time. I rushed into a shower mercifully relieving my lungs.

Stepping out of the shower, anxious to see what I looked like as a blonde, I wrapped a towel around my head, dressed fast, and ran into the bedroom to the big mirror. Removing the towel, I saw the orange of a million carrots on my head.

Horrified at what she'd done, Sally said, "Oh dear. Maybe it should have been two parts peroxide to one part ammonia." My mother and I thanked God for Clairol's dye in burnished autumn.

At the end of eighth grade, I had added Connie to my list of favorite people. She was fun, seeing the humor in almost every situation. Connie was an excellent student and every teacher's pet. I normally didn't like goody-goodies, but she wasn't one of those. She did her work to make the teachers happy, and then she found fun in just about everything else and made me happy.

Connie was a reader. She introduced me to the New York Times bestsellers. Her favorite was *Marjorie Morningstar* by Herman Wouk, which she read for an oral report coming up in English class. I borrowed her book when she was done, but I didn't have enough time to finish it. The day of my book performance, I grabbed her in the hall and explained that I had read all but about the last seventy-five pages. "Tell me how it ends," I begged.

We had to prepare for this bit of perjury in the five minutes allotted for change of classrooms. I had no time to ask questions, so after she related the end of the book to me, I said, "That doesn't make sense." Then I went into class. When my presentation got to Connie's ending, Miss Fisher said, "That doesn't make sense!"

"That's what I told Connie!" I said. She laughed as I confessed I hadn't read to the end. I never finished reading the book; I was so over Marjorie Morningstar.

One day after school, Connie, Sally, and I waited for Mrs. Harmon in her classroom. Sally admired Connie's new dress. I wasn't much interested in clothes, having given up fashion back in Hitchcock, but I coveted her charm bracelet. Every birthday and Christmas, she got a new gold charm for her bracelet, which jingled when she walked, kind of like Mrs. Harmon's keys.

On two windowsills in her classroom, Mrs. Harmon displayed soap sculptures. We'd been assigned to carve fragrant Ivory soap bars into some literary person or thing. The sculptures had been judged, and the winner would be entered into a national competition. I'd sculpted something easy and relatively formless – Moby Dick. Conveniently already white, my Moby looked like a badly mangled bar of Ivory soap. I had to quit working on it soon after I sneezed about a hundred times in a row.

Sally and I were by the windows searching for Sally's sculpture when Connie said, "Oh, y'all, look." She was peering at the school's first-place winner, a tiny white statue of Daughter Eppie from *Silas Marner*, a perfectly carved little figurine with curls, chiseled features, and tiny eyelet ruffles on her dress.

With her thumb and forefinger, Connie lifted the delicate statue. About two inches above the windowsill, the figurine separated at the waist into two pieces. The head and bust lifted in her hand, but the skirt fell back down. Connie's face reflected abject horror! Sally and I didn't even try to stifle a laugh.

"All right," Connie said in a scary no-nonsense whisper. She licked the tiny waist, and placing the dismembered bust back on Eppie's body, quickly rotated her head around like the little girl in *The Exorcist* in a menacing stare at Sally and me. "If either of you ever tells anybody about this before Mrs. Harmon dies, I will kill you. I'm not kidding, Elizabeth!" After threatening our lives several more times, Connie was able to elicit from us a shaky promise just as Mrs. Harmon returned to her classroom, mercifully oblivious to Eppie's demise.

The next day in Latin class, Mrs. Harmon, in a periwinkle blue dress, key ring rattling from the left side of her belt, pulled herself up to her full 5'2" and addressed us.

"CUH-lass!" she said, loudly for emphasis. "VAN-dalism!"

I put my head on my desk and pretended to be asleep. Sally was able to avoid audible laughing by reading and concentrating hard on a dollar bill. When Connie turned and glared at her, Sally stopped smiling.

***

Connor, this past Monday I was discussing the Eppie murder with Sally. She said, "As I remember, we taunted Connie with the threat of telling Mrs. Harmon. I think you raised your hand in class at least once, saying, 'Mrs. Harmon, there's something I've been wanting to tell you...' and then you related something innocuous. Connie was sure you were going to tell Mrs. Harmon who mangled Eppie."

Latin

At times my father would quiz me, asking what I was learning at school. One day in the spring of my sophomore year, we met in the hallway. He was dressed in khaki pants and a faded plaid shirt; around his middle, a canvas apron contained nails and screws and a place to loop his hammer.

When I told Daddy I was planning to take two years of Latin, he refused to sign off on it. His reasoning went something like this... "Latin is dead and of no use today. You need to be able to support yourself, and Latin won't contribute anything to your bottom line. Therefore, you should take typing and shorthand."

I'd already taken typing, so I wrote *shorthand* on the official form. He signed the card, and the next day I erased *shorthand* and wrote *Latin I*. I took two years of Latin, making sure I never mentioned it again.

When I was fifteen, I was able to get a driver's license under a special "hardship rule." We lived in one town, I went to school in another, and my father worked in still another. Uncle Ralph talked to a judge in Galveston about getting me a special license to drive. With only one car, it was a hardship for my depressed mother to drive my father to Texas City, then backtrack to La Marque High School, and then back to Hitchcock. In the afternoon, she reversed the process: drive to La Marque to get me, then to Texas City to get my father, and then home.

Still wearing my red fuzzy slippers, I drove my father to work in Texas City each day, back tracked to La Marque High School, and changed into my regular shoes. At the end of the school day, I went home with Sally and Connie to do homework until it was time to go to Texas City to pick up my father, then home, leaving Mama unencumbered.

One unhappy day at school, I couldn't find the car keys. Sally and I searched. Nothing. We walked to her house. I was already running late to pick up my father when her daddy drove me to Texas City to get him. Daddy was walking down the highway when we found him, furious. Fortunately, he had a spare key to the car with him. Mr. Miller left us at the high school parking lot, and I dreaded the ride home. I knew I was in big trouble.

Daddy fumed angrily all the way back to Hitchcock, puffed up like an adder. When we got home, Mama was cooking dinner. Daddy blew in, sloshing his anger all over the kitchen. Mama didn't join his fury at first, saying, "Now, Richard, everyone makes mistakes."

However, he pushed her until she, too, lost it.

"She didn't just lose the car key," he said. "She also lost the house key, the barn key, the church key..."

"Well, I'll be God damn!" Mama said. Now both of them were mad at me. I said I had homework and escaped to my room, preferring Latin by a mile to staying in the kitchen with my parents.

Not long after the keys debacle, my father bought himself a new pickup truck to replace me. I continued to drive the '53 Ford to school. My friends christened it "the green pea."

Having my own wheels was a mixed blessing. Something called the bendix switch was faulty, causing the engine to fail when stopped at a red light or stop sign. The only way I could start it again was to take the engine out of overdrive, put the standard transmission into reverse, and make all my passengers get out and "rock the car" backwards. It became a usual sight for people stopped at a red light to see a load of teenage girls in various getups, including red fluffy house shoes, hop out and go to the front of the car to push.

I usually left school unlawfully at lunchtime and went to the Pioneer Drive-In for lunch. They had a special of hamburger, French fries, and a Coke for 35 cents. Before long, Jane and a few others joined me. We hurried through eating and made it back in time for the start of the next class.

Sometimes Jane and I would sneak into the auditorium and go upstairs to the projection room to smoke cigarettes during lunch. The principal, Mr. Schlegelmilch, also came into the auditorium, but he stayed downstairs in the restroom. We assumed he was taking a smoke break, too.

Teachers

My worst subject was Latin. I should have listened to my father! He warned me Latin was dead and useless. While boredom was the reason I failed sixth grade geography, and lack of long division and the times tables explained my ignorance of mathematics, my experience with Latin was, how you say in English, a different ballgame. I had always been interested in language, but I had to add Latin to the growing list of subjects about which I was clueless. Over my last two years in high school, I became sure this dead language had committed suicide.

Connor, Latin is an inflected language, while English is a word-order language. English subjects in declarative sentences appear just before the verb. Latin, on the other hand, sprinkles nouns and verbs willy-nilly in the sentence and inflects [ends] them with declensions and conjugations, expecting us to know who did what and to whom. No wonder the language died.

One day at a time – for about a thousand of Aunt Jewel's dog years – I puzzled over Latin I and II. I found Latin vocabulary much easier to learn than the grammar. Since my only study skill was memorizing, I mastered about a million Latin words and used those words to help me figure out Latin sentences. It didn't go well.

I kept losing my textbook. Something Freudian there! The first time, my mother gave me five dollars to pay for it. When it happened again, Dee Dee, Mama's best friend, gave me money and promised not to tell. When I lost it a third time, I was on my own. During lunch for three days, I panhandled in the hall between classes and raised the money in nickels and dimes to replace it. I was able to hang on to the third copy. In the 1950s, $5.00 was like $25 today.

Mrs. Harmon, the Latin teacher, was something of a mystery to me. Built like a fire plug, she had a ring of keys hanging from her belt, jingling with her every move. Connie called her the chatelaine of La Marque High School. You could hear her coming a while before you saw her. She looked to be about 5'2". I couldn't tell how old Mrs. Harmon was, but she was not as old as Miss Jones, the history teacher.

Connie thought Mrs. Harmon read professional journals because in Latin II, she tried out the latest in classroom management strategies. For example, she began dictation as soon as the bell rang, hoping to teach "bell to bell." You'd think we'd learn to enter her room and get out our papers and pens; however, getting ready for class before the tardy bell rang didn't ever occur to me. When Mrs. Harmon began to dictate, I dived for my chair and grabbed a blank sheet of paper off a friend's desk to get it all down.

I was a good speller; my last misspelled word in school was *language*, marked wrong in the low-fourth grade in Huntsville. At the end of each high school year, the principal bestowed on me the National Office Management Association, or NOMA, award for spelling. All you had to do was correctly spell 100 words taken from a larger list. I didn't often look at the larger list but trusted I could spell the NOMA words as well as any others. Preparation for anything was not my forte. It still isn't.

Each day, Connie and Sally dutifully entered the Latin classroom and got out their papers and pencils before class started. When I finally got settled with paper, pencil, and desk, I did well on the dictation. I could spell Latin words correctly, but I never elevated my understanding to the sentence level. After Mrs. Harmon taught us some sounds of Latin letters, I developed an admirable fluency in reading the Latin text aloud. However, I could see two problems:

- First, although it sounded like I knew what I was reading, I hadn't a clue.

- Second, how did Mrs. Harmon know what sounds the letters represented if she'd never heard a native Latin speaker?

A dark day dawned when Mrs. Harmon was gung-ho about a new Latin achievement test. *Oh, Jesus,* I thought. Now she'll find out I don't know any Latin and have no achievement to measure. My worst nightmare had come upon me! For almost a year I had been able to look and sound like I knew a lot more than Latin vocabulary.

"Just do your best; this won't count on your grade." As she passed out the answer sheets and test booklets, I bowed my head and cast my eyes down to my black and white saddle oxfords. I felt doomed to ignominious exposure as a Latin-language fraud.

We didn't hear anything about our test results for a few weeks, so I began to relax. Then one Monday morning, Mrs. Harmon entered the classroom, dropped an armload of papers on her desk, announced she had the achievement test scores, and she did not look happy.

"CUH-lass, somebody made two percentile," she said in strident gravitas. I strongly suspected I was the stupid one.

I wilted. *Oh my God, I'm dead! I'll fail Latin, and my Daddy will be mad! Mama will kill me.* Then I looked at my score: seventy percentile! I couldn't believe it. Mrs. Harmon said fifty percentile was average. I had guessed my way to twenty points above average. Of course, Connie and Sally were at the top of the class in the 90s. Another girl scored the two, only to be removed from Latin and placed in another class. I found it hard to believe she knew less Latin than I.

Another day Mrs. Harmon announced a new strategy for better learning management: henceforth we students, not she the teacher, would begin reciting the Latin declensions when the bell rang. As usual Connie and Sally began their A+ recitation on time: *hic, haic, hoc, huius, huius, huius,* and so on. I memorized those declensions and joined everyone else sounding like a pig rooting for truffles.

Connie suspected Mrs. Harmon thought Sally was Jewish. The day before Yom Kippur, she asked Sally if she would be in school the next day. Sally said she would be there. Then in November, Mrs. Harmon worried about Sally's parents and whether they would approve of her being in the Christmas pageant. Sally assured her she had permission.

Connie said Mrs. Harmon thought Sally was Jewish because [a] she had dark hair and eyes, and [b] her last name was Miller, as in Schreiber and Miller Furniture Store in Galveston. "Schreiber" was Jewish so "Miller" must have been also. Therefore, Mrs. Harmon thought Sally was Jewish, too.

American History

Our history teacher looked like she belonged in a comic book teaching Veronica, Betty, Archie and Jughead about American Colonial history. Tall and thin and wrinkled, Miss Jones parted her gray hair in the middle and swept it into a bun on the back of her neck.

Here's the thing: Miss Jones did not like Connie, who was usually every teacher's pet. Unlike Mrs. Harmon, who showered Connie with kudos *ad nauseum*, Miss Jones suspected Connie was a Republican. We couldn't figure out why, but Miss Jones was very old, so we cut her a lot of slack. She loved Sally and me because we attended her church and because I pretended to be a Democrat.

Miss Jones tried to interest my mother in singing in the Methodist Church choir. By reminding her of my mother's beautiful soprano voice, I dangled that carrot before her nose every once in a while. My mother's voice had been the solo in every church we'd gone to. For some reason, when we got to La Marque, Mama hung her choir robe on a nail in her mind and retired.

Miss Jones had just one teaching strategy: outline the book, which didn't work with my method of memorizing. From the start, she and I were not a good fit. Thinking the class didn't have enough sense to get the outline right, she dictated it to us. Then the rest of the week she helped us fill the outline with facts. We knew Miss Jones never graded our outlines because Jane and I wrote notes about boys to fill the blank spaces. All parts of the outline with writing came back with an A and a stamp of Miss Jones' approval.

Occasionally, to change things up, Miss Jones read a little story to us, like *Wind in the Willows*, but I usually missed the point of the story, assuming there was one. And another thing: Miss Jones led us in prayer before she gave us the test questions. I gratefully used those few extra prayer minutes to memorize more history.

SAN ANTONIO

A speech competition in San Antonio at Trinity University each spring offered us a rare chance at a school-sponsored trip. Prospective contestants were required to undergo rigorous tryouts. In eleventh grade, Sally entered the radio broadcast category, while the rest of us competed in poetry interpretation.

Jane chose James Weldon Johnson's "The Creation" for her entry. It would have sounded better had she sported a hefty bass voice, but she did a creditable job. The poem is so beautiful, it really doesn't need help. Connie selected "My Last Duchess" by Robert Browning, brutal irony revealing an evil, malignant persona.

Jo Ann interpreted Edna St. Vincent Millay's "Patterns," which I didn't fully understand at the time. The first line was clear enough: "I walked down the garden paths and all the daffodils were blooming." Somewhere in the middle of the poem, I got confused by the pattern metaphor.

Never a good interpreter of poetry, I chose an interminable singsong, "Maud Muller" by John Greenleaf Whittier. Written mid-19th century, the poem has about a million rhyming couplets and tells the story of a young aristocrat and a farm maid who see each other one time and yearn the rest of their lives for a relationship forbidden by the class system of the time. The rhythm and rhyme scheme lulled me and my audience into a mindless trance. I think I chose it because it was so long, and I was a stellar memorizer. I figure I won because the judge's mind strayed off topic for a long time, and I was still reciting when her attention returned to me about fifteen minutes later.

All four of us earned a place in the school contest, but we didn't want to win anything in San Antonio because then our time would be taken up with semi-finals and finals in the various competitions.

In San Antonio, a lottery schedule arranged Jane and me in the same presentation session. We arrived at the location at the appointed time and found two chairs side by side in the crowded room. I should have known this situation was not propitious; Jane and I had a track record of misbehaving.

The third contestant walked to the front of the classroom and announced she was going to recite "Patterns" by Edna St. Vincent Millay. Jo Ann's poem. a tall girl with a friendly face sprinkled with freckles across her nose, red hair in pigtail braids, she reminded me of a Raggedy Ann doll.

Connor, I know I have no right to find fault with someone else's Texas accent, but I'm going to do it anyway. She had an exaggerated, loud drawl sounding something like, "I wauk down the garden payz..." It was one of those surprise situations where you absolutely cannot laugh, and where you absolutely cannot avoid laughing. To cover any audible slip I made, I did a fake cough and put my head down on my desk. Jane took a page from Sally's book and studied a dollar bill.

When Raggedy Ann finished her presentation, Jane and I excused ourselves, ran out into the hall, and laughed our heads off as quietly as we could. Then we didn't go back in together. I stayed outside the room while she presented, and she did the same for me.

Getting back to the motel room after it was over, Jane, Sally, Connie, and I smoked an essential cigarette to calm our nerves and discuss the contest. We were in mid-puff when Jo Ann knocked on our locked door. We snuffed the Pall Malls and fanned the air to dissipate the smoky fog in the room. Jo Ann kept yelling to let her in. *Busted!* We listened again to her sermon about smoking: it's unhealthy, expensive, and gives the wrong impression to others of who we are. We were afraid to smoke the rest of the trip.

My Playground

As you have probably already recognized, high school was my playground. I took very little seriously, whether classes, teachers, or other students. I don't know how it happened – I wouldn't have voted for me – but I was elected treasurer of the student council my senior year. As a result of my elevated position, I was awarded an hour in the library for council business. One day, as Miss White opened the library first thing in the morning, I entered the big room first and spotted all four of her goldfish stapled to the bulletin board. I don't remember laughing, but I'm sure my initial reaction lacked sufficient sympathy to keep Miss White from thinking I did it. Of course, I didn't do it. I valued a fish's life almost more than I valued my own. I was incapable of being cruel to helpless goldfish.

I continued my love of language, serene in the confines of the library. However, my favorite poems took a turn toward the dark. "Invictus" became a favorite.

> Out of the night that covers me,
> black as the pit from pole to pole,
> I thank whatever gods there be
> for my unconquerable soul.

Although I didn't think I had a great soul, I knew the black pit. I lived in loneliness nightly in bed and daily in the sunlight. I was living in another town from my friends who burst with excitement over the boys who phoned them. My number was long distance. So was my heart.

I acted much younger than my age in school, running in the halls and talking in a loud voice. My behavior was most likely the reason I had no boyfriends. A few of the premium high school boys did call and invite me to the movies, but I was terrified and found it hard to talk to them.

I basked in "The Raven." In "Philosophy of Composition," Edgar Allen Poe calls the emotion "the luxury of sorrow," citing the persona in "The Raven," who knows the word *nevermore* is the answer to all his grieving questions of the lost Lenore. The raven flies into his chamber amid an explosion of black feathers and settles on the "pallid bust of Pallas," a goddess believed to be wisdom itself. Finally turning his attention to the black bird, the scholar wonders why the bird keeps saying, "Nevermore." Then he knows each repetition of the word will stab him, giving voice to his abject grief. He experiences a most perverse relief. He finally asks the question of the "thing of evil:" whether he'll ever see the lost Lenore again.

Nevermore.

Near hysteria, he commands the bird, "Take thy beak from out my heart and take thy form from off my door!" At the end, he realizes he is to live in the shadow thrown on the floor by the raven. *Will I ever be free*, he wonders, and of course his answer is... *nevermore.*

One of the duties of the student council treasurer was to collect the nickels out of the Coke machines. I had a rap sheet with Coke nickels, so I didn't object when Miss White said I had to empty the coins in the presence of the council's vice president. I guessed she didn't trust me. I didn't trust me, either. Each day the vice president and I gathered the money from all the Coke machines and counted it in the library. Unfortunately, the vice president had the same problem with nickels I had earlier overcome. He filled his pockets before we got back to Miss White's watchful eye. I scrutinized him closely to prevent his stealing, but a couple of times he got by with it. On those occasions when our nickel total dropped, I'm sure by the way she looked at me Miss White thought I was stealing the money.

For our senior project, Miss Jones tried an experiment for lessons in American democracy: The senior class, all 123 of us, would hold an election. We had two political parties, which we named the Dixie party and the Lone Star party. Each senior chose the party he or she wanted to affiliate with. I don't know how it happened, but Sally and I ended up in the Dixie party with boring people, and Connie and everyone else we liked were in Lone Star.

We held mock conventions to appoint our slate of candidates. Sally was nominated fire chief, and I was nominated alderman on the city council. I didn't even know what *alderman* meant. Miss Jones lectured to us about smoke-filled rooms and how nominations were made at the national level. However, the only smoke-filled room in our election occurred in one of our big rallies.

One afternoon we in the Dixie party rallied in the auditorium, trying to think of some way to beat up the Lone Star party, who were rallying in the cafeteria, thinking of ways to destroy us. The Lone Stars, however, were ahead of us in planned annihilation and left their space to descend on us for the purpose of disrupting our rally.

A few of our Dixiecrat crybabies ran to complain to Miss Jones, who had not predicted this unhappy situation. While she tried to decide what to do, the confrontation got louder. I looked up to see the auditorium doors open, and in marched all the Lone Stars. Some on our side started pushing the invaders back toward the hall, fists flying. I moved farther back in the auditorium to get a better vantage point. There was a lot of noise, people yelling, cursing. A Lone Star member started banging on a drum smuggled out of the band hall to lead the Lone Star parade, adding some extra noise to the situation.

We really needed uniforms because it was hard to remember who was on our side. One of the marchers bonked somebody over the head with a campaign poster stick, and another student jabbed his poster into a Dixie chest and belly, and the Civil War was once again upon us.

The next thing was, *please dear God no*, we smelled smoke. One of our Dixie pundits, using his own personal Zippo lighter, had set fire to a Lone Star campaign sign. Miss Jones and one of the Lone Stars smothered the flames with a jacket before anything else started to burn. Hoping to appear innocent of malfeasance, most of the Lone Star rioters made a strategic retreat to the cafeteria, where they were supposed to be in the first place.

Teachers on our end of the hall came into the auditorium to see what was going on. I didn't get to hear what Mr. Schegelmilch yelled at Miss Jones because other teachers sent us back to whatever classroom we were usually in at 2:00. It was exciting and interesting for a little while, but back in her classroom, Miss Jones was frazzled and close to crying.

One beautiful spring day Miss White assigned the student council officers a rare task. The three of us were to go to Houston to a flag company and buy a replacement for the school's old, somewhat shredded flag. Arlene, the student council president, drove us the thirty or so miles to our destination, where we viewed flags of every size and price range. Choosing an appropriate flag for our high school pole, we took our purchase to the car and opened the bag to admire its contents. Then our vice president pulled from under his jacket a flag he'd stolen. Not at all surprised by this development, the president and I forced him to take it back and leave it there.

Miss White continued to consider the president and vice president paragons of honesty. However, she didn't trust me one bit. She had sized me up well early on, but she couldn't prove anything.

Operator

After the eleventh grade, I worked as a long-distance telephone operator in Galveston. The application process was simple: fill out an application and take a spelling test. Right down my alley. The words on the telephone company test were more difficult than other tests I had taken because they were names of cities. Included were Mexia [Ma-hay-ah], Nacogdoches [Na-ka-doe-chez], Natchitoches [Nak-i-tush], and other puzzlers. I spelled them all correctly. During the summer I worked full time at $1.10 per hour. Later, in September I went to half-time. I had to quit in January because work was taking up too much of my senior year.

The work was easy. Years before touch dialing became the norm for long distance, operators placed those calls on a rotary dialer. We had special pencils with balls on the end of them to spare our fingers, and we wore head gear plugged into circuits and sat on stools high off the floor in a line in front of a huge floor-to-ceiling switchboard.

In 1956, Southwestern Bell technology was different from our phone service today. Only operators could place long-distance calls. The switchboard lit each incoming call all the way down the line, to be answered on the back cord by an operator. The front cords were for completing the calls. However, we could accept money only on the back cord, so we had to answer the light with the front cord when a pay phone was involved. Then we looked in a book for how much to charge. There weren't a lot of those calls, and it was easy to switch cords from back to front. I made a game of trying to get all six of my "lights" busy and keeping them lit. I was the darling of the supervisors.

For mobile service in cars and mobile marine in boats, there were different instructions. We had to answer each call with front cords and dial on back ones after consulting references in books laid on top of the switchboard. I never fully understood how it all worked, so I asked the supervisors to assign me to plain long-distance positions on the board, if possible.

The one time I was placed on mobile service/marine was a debacle in the making. I begged the operator next to me to take the calls coming in because I didn't know how. She agreed just as mobile service winked on. She answered it, but then mobile marine flickered. I had to answer it. Nervous and shaking, I flipped my pencil up in the air before it fell to the floor.

"Mobile marine," I said, looking around for another pencil.

A man's voice struggled through wind and boat engine noise to reel off about a thousand numbers and letters. "This is W856SA 293..." on and on. I had to unhook myself from the switchboard, step off the high seat, pick up my pencil from the floor, climb back up to my chair, and plug into the switchboard again. This I did as fast as I could, and when I returned, the caller was finishing his destination number with "Over."

"Will you repeat that, sir?" I said.

"Goddam, operator!"

"I know, sir, but I dropped my pencil." He repeated the numbers, and I was able to complete his connection.

Answering the information calls was almost as scary. If we were asked to find a number for another city, we called the city's information operator, a person set up on a special switchboard like ours. Once my caller said, "Operator, how are things in sin city?" referring to the open gambling and sex industries of Galveston. Sometimes we had to consult a big book for routing instructions to rural areas. Meanwhile, if a Galveston caller wanted a Galveston number, we provided it free of charge.

Most of the time it was a fun job. I listened to pieces of conversations when we weren't busy, like a call from George Zaharias in Galveston to Phil Harris in Hollywood, both celebrities, to announce the death at the UT Medical Branch in Galveston of his wife, the famous golfer Babe Zaharias. She had been suffering from colon cancer, and we operators passed the news down the line each time we took a call from him giving an update on his wife's condition.

    I stayed with the phone company until Christmas. Because I was going to school all day and working three nights a week, I was tired. I quit until after senior year, when I needed a summer job again, so I'd have a good excuse for not going to stay two weeks with Fran and Carl in Pasadena Hell.

SAT

Graduation was coming up! My father had the "college talk" with me early in my senior year. Sentenced to higher education by the Court of Parental Expectations, I learned from Connie and Sally that the Scholastic Aptitude Test was required for entrance to most colleges. Therefore, I applied to take the SAT, given in Galveston at Ball High School. I did great on the verbal parts of the test, thanks to English grammar and my store of Latin words and word parts. However, the mathematics sections were torture.

Remember, Connor, I skipped the multiplication tables and long division. For the entire time I spent on mathematics in the SAT, I thought I had wandered into the first circle of Dante's Hell: "Abandon Hope, All Who Enter Here." There were questions about planting how many beans how many inches apart in a garden with how many rows ten feet long. *Who cares?* I thought. *Just buy a bunch of beans and put them in the ground until you run out of either beans or rows. Easy problem to solve.* I felt a migraine coming on.

One question told of a plane and a train leaving at the same time from New York both heading for Chicago, the plane flying over the train at some point in the trip. I think the question asked us to calculate how far they had gone when the plane was over the train. My first thought was, *Who wants to go to Chicago?* Then a consideration of trains and planes further derailed my focus. I couldn't figure out why someone would choose the train, since obviously the plane would get there faster. However, you had more room on a train, even a bunk to sleep in, so maybe trains were better after all if you weren't in a hurry.

And besides, I was kind of scared of flying. I think I left the question blank.

Going to college didn't scare me. I was always thinking of some way to get away from my sister and her groper husband, my parents and Godawful allergenic, asthmatic, humid, air-polluted Galveston County.

I wanted to go to an Ivy League university because of their beautiful campuses. Tall and thin, I would wear woolen clothes to keep me warm. I could picture myself walking into an ivy-covered library. All winter I would slosh through snow, a tortured and unhappy soul, enjoying dark, depressing literature. However, putting a blow torch to my icy fantasy, Daddy said I had to stay in Texas for in-state tuition.

Connie said she was going to the University of Texas. She was so sure of herself and certain of everything. I decided to stick with her; after all, she had been a huge influence on my high school performance. Unfortunately, not everyone agreed UT was a good fit for me. Some of my teachers thought I would lose much of my personal identity. I had no personal identity!

My parents were delighted with my choice, but the University of Texas registrar was not. In fact, since I was in the second quarter of my graduating class with a 92 average, UT advised against it. I figured my mathematics scores on the SAT betrayed me and prejudiced the admissions people, but I was willing to give it a go anyway. I just wouldn't take any math courses. Besides, if I flunked out, it would at least be from a top-tier university.

Toward the end of my senior year, the high school counselor, Mrs. Williamson, talked with me. Her office was small and sterile, neither bookshelves nor books, nor bulletin board, in fact, nothing of interest in the room, including her. She dressed in a dark, ill-fitting suit.

"What are your plans after graduating, Elizabeth?"

"I'm planning to go to college," I said.

"Which one?" she asked.

"The University of Texas."

Taking a deep breath, and most likely looking at my SAT score and second-quarter grades on her desk, she said, "Why not go to a junior college?"

"My daddy won't let me."

"Then a smaller state school like Sam Houston State Teachers College?"

A quick memory of my life in Huntsville stabbed through my heart like a knife. "I'm going where Connie is going, to Austin."

She looked at me over her glasses. Then squinting as if she'd been reading a cloudy crystal-ball, she said, "You won't make it."

I said nothing. To a girl who's trying to insert suicide into her daily schedule, failing at the University of Texas isn't super scary.

When I told my friends I planned to go to Austin, some said, "It's so big you'll just be a number." I thought about that a lot. I was not convinced being just a number was a bad thing if you were me. I liked the idea of going to class and remaining an unknown, judged only on achievement, and not on my pitiful self. I could accept it if I failed to achieve. I just didn't want anyone seeing my other deficiencies. And besides, if things got too tough, I could always kill myself.

JEAN LAFITTE

In our senior year, Sally and I thought we'd apply for a summer job in the Galveston tourism industry. She got one on the beach at the Seahorse Hotel, where she took orders for room service for the restaurant. The downtown Hotel Jean LaFitte hired me as both desk clerk and hotel switchboard operator.

It was 1957, the year Will Wilson and his band of Texas Rangers shut down illegal gambling on the Island. Sally and I were seventeen years old. When I worked the 3:00 to 11:00 shift, I saw the Rangers, outfitted in their Western uniforms including Stetson hats and cowboy boots. Headquartered at the Jean LaFitte, they left the hotel around 6:00 P.M. with axes in their hands. They returned about 10:00. The next day, we would read in the *Galveston Morning News* an account of their raids. Once when I worked 3:00-11:00 and was back the next day for 7:00-3:00, a Ranger asked, "Do you ever go home?"

The next day's *Galveston Morning News* reported each raid and how many slot machines and other illicit gambling paraphernalia had been destroyed.

To save the time and expense of a commute, Sally and I spent the summer with Aunt Lou Lou, who had bought a house on 17th Street, about six blocks from the Jean LaFitte and ten blocks from the beach. The house was a two-story affair looking older than it was because of humidity and salt from the Gulf climate. A beautiful wooden staircase led from the entry hall to the second floor. Unaccustomed to stairs, either Sally or I stumbled down them at least once a week.

During this time, I was glad to be busy and away from my clingy boyfriend. We had a date planned one evening in my seventeenth summer, but I got a better offer. Lou Lou advised against breaking my date, but a friend needed another girl for a blind date with a freshman from UT. I sick-called my boyfriend, who unexpectedly showed up earlier than my date, to see if I was all right. I told him I was going out with someone else. Why would he ever want anything to do with me after such disrespect? However, perhaps thinking marriage would cement our relationship, he began to beg me to marry him. I said NO.

INTO THE BREACH

Come September, I was ready to go to Austin. Well, as ready as you can be with no self-confidence. I don't know what I had spent my money on, but it wasn't clothes. Half-expecting to flunk out, I planned to say goodbye to the miserable humidity and heat of Galveston County.

My preparations for Austin are something of a fog. I'd never been far from home, and I knew nothing about independent living. I procrastinated too long; Blanton and other close-to-campus dormitories were filled. However, I found a beautiful dormitory faintly resembling an ivy-league building – but without the ivy – about a mile from campus on top of a hill: Kirby Hall. I was blissfully ignorant of how hard it is to walk two or three miles and then climb a steep hill when you grew up lazy at sea level.

I got a footlocker because everyone I knew going to college got a footlocker; however, I should have spent the money on a wardrobe to go into it. As it was, I was prepared to go to Austin with pitifully few clothes in my locker and a sizable measure of something like root rot in my mind.

In 1957 at age seventeen, I had become a person who rarely followed directions, knew better than the experts, and probed every situation for something, anything, entertaining. This is the person I carried off to Austin, the largest [at the time] university in the Southwest and maybe in the whole country. Painfully aware of my academic shortcomings, I was prepared to fail, but I didn't allow myself to dwell on it.

Students today have no concept of the logistics of registering 35,000 students for each semester without computers. The short version is for each prospective student to design a course of study and complete innumerable forms, submitting them separately to various departments. After all the deadlines are met in this preliminary phase, we were ready to begin.

At this point, I had questions. Yikes! What will I major in? I searched my brain: *What, if anything, am I good at?* My answer was, *I can read and write. Well, maybe not write right since I don't know anything.* Lacking original ideas, I found a tiny shred of positivity in my pretty handwriting, and I was a good speller. I was fairly confident I could write any ideas occurring to me; after all, I was planning to attend the University of Texas, the birthplace of ideas. However, considering my present limited knowledge, I tried to picture a career after graduation. I couldn't imagine anyone paying me to sit around and read books, but some people are paid to write. So, journalism would be my declared major.

Examining required courses listed in the catalog for a journalism degree, I realized right there I was screwed before I started. I had to take another language. Latin, I knew, was out of the question – I had no desire to exhume the corpse again. Some languages didn't even use the alphabet, so my pretty handwriting and NOMA spelling awards would be useless in, say, Greek.

I asked my cousin Jean which language she had taken. "German is pretty easy," she said. I could never trust her about what was easy because she thought algebra was easy. However, no one else I knew had taken a language outside of Latin. I had never heard one word spoken in German, except *Gesundheit*. I got depressed when I glanced through Jean's text. *Jesus, help me!*

I thought English and American history were do-able. At least they would be presented in words I could spell. Biology, also written in English, was next, a two-semester course of botany and zoology. The last journalism requirement for first semester was algebra. *Yikes!* I hoped Boyfriend, a mechanical engineering major, could help me from the first day of class. [Turns out he was no magician.]

Registration for the fall semester at UT Austin took place in Gregory Gym on several days in July. The registrar assigned each student to an appointment; my time was 12:00 High Noon. It was about a thousand degrees when I joined the line of nooners snaking out of the gym and down several blocks. The papers in my hands were getting sweat wet, and I could imagine myself crawling into the gym, tongue swollen out of my mouth, hand at my throat.

The person ahead of me, Bob, didn't appear to be suffering from the heat although he admitted it was warm, and he was glad he'd worn his baseball cap to shade his eyes from the Texas sun. The temperature had passed warm when it reached 95 degrees at ten o'clock, and I had no baseball cap.

Bob was a civil engineering major and was excited about the coming semester. I shared my nascent journalism plans with him and just stood there waiting either to faint or die of thirst. Suddenly a man stepped out of the air-conditioned gym, lifted a megaphone to his mouth, and yelled, "All English majors can come on through."

A quick catalog check showed the journalism and English first semesters required the same courses. Mentally tossing my journalism degree into the air like so much confetti, I happily stepped out of the line and headed for the gym.

"You're not an English major," Bob said.

"I am now," I said. "I'll change back to journalism next semester."

The cool air inside the gym revived me some. Greeting us English majors as we entered the gym, several volunteers showed the way to the sectionizers, who bestowed course cards marked with a class section number. Those cards were the ticket into a particular section of a class. Only one section of all the classes I had chosen was open. Thank God it was algebra, MWF ten o'clock, the same section Boyfriend was in. The rest of the sections I had chosen were closed.

Finding other classes I could join, without involving Saturdays, was the biggest chore of all. All the good times of the classes were reserved for something called Plan II. After being turned down for a seat in about ten different sections of all my required courses, it was apparent I would have to attend class at 8:00 a.m. on Saturdays unless I joined Plan II.

Good news! The UT catalog listed first semester Plan II courses the same as the English requirements. I erased the numbers assigned by the sectionizers and penciled in the best times for the classes. Plan II was proving to be a snap. Paying my $50 tuition and another $50 fee for labs, and parking – I had no car – I was now registered. Boyfriend and I drove the four hours back to La Marque to await the move to Austin and the beginning of classes. I didn't know enough to be frightened.

Come September, I was ready to go to UT. Well, as ready as you can be with no wardrobe and no self-confidence.

Half expecting to flunk out, I said goodbye to the miserable humidity and heat in Galveston County and La Marque and hello to the miserable heat and humidity in Travis County and Austin. I took with me a huge fever blister right at the end of my nose.

And it came to pass, as they say in the Bible, the first week of classes finally arrived. I had skipped the real first week because it was orientation and not required. What was I thinking? God forbid I get some information on where to go and how to get there. I had a Monday morning biology lab at 8:00.

Kirby Hall, as I said, was at the top of a hill about a mile from the English Building on the "40 Acres." A three-story red brick with stately columns in the front, the dormitory looked more comfortable than it turned out to be. The house mother called a meeting on Sunday night to distribute a comprehensive list of the rules of the house. The first rule was no one was to use the elevator unless they were carrying something big and heavy. I moaned; my room was on the third floor.

Standing next to me was one of the prettiest girls I had ever seen outside of the movies. Her name tag said, "Hi, I'm Sally."

As beautiful as Jane, New Sally's striking red hair framed her face, cleft chin as pronounced as Ava Gardner's, and very white skin. My nose and I stood next to her on the first evening meeting feeling not only ugly, but also diseased. There was no hiding the fever blister and no forgetting about it because I could see it when I looked straight ahead. I resolved to peacefully coexist with my nose.

I whispered to her, "I wonder how long it's going to take me to break every one of these rules."

"Let's break them in order," she said. I had found Nirvana! Someone who thought like me. For the rest of the year, my new Sally and I worked our way through the thirty rules. There were admonishments about having wastepaper [or other detritus] in your waste basket, being on the phone more than three minutes, failing to observe quiet hours, coming in on time, and being late for lunch.

Where else would you put wastepaper? Punishment for breaking the rules was imprisonment, not being allowed to leave Kirby Hall except for class. The penultimate rule was we were not to have alcohol in our rooms, and the last was no men could be on our floor. At the end of the spring semester, we had those two rules left to break. New Sally smuggled two bottles of beer up to the third floor. We waited till everyone was asleep, went into a bathroom stall to drink it, and then put the bottles down the trash chute, which incidentally ran right next to the house mother's bedroom. *BANG, CRASH,* all the way down to the basement. Then we hurried to get into our beds and pretended to be asleep. Sure enough, less than five minutes passed before my room door opened, checking to see if I was still up. I'm sure Housemother knew it was I. The next day, Sally's boyfriend sneaked up to the third floor. He didn't stay long, and then he sneaked back out. Oh, dear, I got ahead of the story again.

Week one of classes. It had rained for several days, covering most of the ground on campus in puddles. Early Monday morning, behind the Biology Building, the lawns looked like I imagined Venice, water crisscrossed with walkways. The building was almost deserted on this first day of business. My lab was listed in the catalog for 8:00 on Mondays, but I couldn't find it. Walking down a long hall, I was hoping to see labs in action. I met up with someone walking the same hall in the basement.

Looking at him, I realized he was the wettest person in the world. Austin rain had done a number on him, but I pretended I didn't notice.

"Did you know there is a pond behind the building?" he said.

"Yes," I said.

"I thought it was just another puddle inside the walkway, so I decided to cut across the grass to get in out of the rain."

Cutting across the lawn had led him, expecting only a few inches of rainwater, to step off the sidewalk to the bottom of the pond where biologists grew their fungi and other scum. Thank heavens it wasn't too deep, so he crawled out of the pond like a primordial creature, suede jacket seeping water like a sponge, and resumed the search for his biology class. I couldn't wait to tell Connie.

I found a biology class and went in and sat down. After about ten minutes of not understanding a word, I left.

Unable to find my biology lab, my fever blister and I headed with dread and fear to the Mathematics Building for my 10:00 algebra class to meet Boyfriend. There I learned that labs didn't meet in the first week of classes. I should have gone to Orientation.

The Second Circle of Hell

I cannot describe to you how scared I was. Boyfriend and I found desks toward the back of the room. I think about 60 students were in the algebra class, mostly Chinese. When the professor came in, he said the first 250 pages of the text were review and if there were no questions, we would skip them. *WHAT? WAIT!*

"Ask a question," I told Boyfriend.

"No," he said. "I know this."

Desperate, I raised my hand, and the professor acknowledged me.

"Yes," he said. "Which problem?"

I wanted to yell *ALL OF THEM!* Instead, I let my gaze fall into the open book and grabbed a problem.

"Number 128," I said.

"Okay," he said, "Read it to me."

Connor, have there ever been moments in your life you wish you could take back, things you've done which haunt you? I was so scared I forgot how to read exponents. I began to read the problem.

"3X with a little, tiny 4 on top of it," I said.

Then about 50 Asian students in front of me turned around in their seats to get a better look at the village idiot. I managed to live through reading the problem with all the "X-es and Y-s and their little, tiny numbers up on top," sure the Chinese were thinking Americans are stupid.

Boyfriend pushed the text onto my desk and moved his desk farther away. I was traumatized! The first rattle out of the box, and I had demonstrated how ignorant I was. I couldn't wait to escape the classroom. I didn't hear any of the professor's explanation of how to solve the problem. Cheeks burning from embarrassment, I could think of nothing other than getting out of there.

At the end of the class, I told Boyfriend I was going to the dean's office to drop algebra.

"You have to take it," he argued. "It's required for your degree."

I said, steadfast, "If I get close to graduation, however unlikely, I'll take algebra. If I flunk out, I don't want death by mathematics."

The office of the Dean of the College of Arts and Sciences was in the Tower Building, which J. Frank Dobie, an iconic Texas writer, said resembled "... a toothpick in a pie." About a dozen people stood around the secretary's desk, and another five or six sat in chairs along a wall. Phones ringing, people going in and out, chaos ruled.

"The dean is meeting with sco-pro students today. Are you on scholastic probation?" the secretary asked, looking at my nose and brushing a wisp of hair out of her face with her hand.

"Not yet," I said.

"If you decide to wait for him, just know he has to talk to most of these students ahead of you. Or you can come back tomorrow," she said, looking hopeful to get rid of me. However, as I said, I was determined, not wanting to see any of those algebra people ever again. Dropping the class was my only option, apart from suicide. However, even in all my pain of being stupid, I suspected suicide would be overkill. Connor, please excuse the pun.

I waited about an hour and a half in the dean's outer office. When the last probationary student left, Dean Burdine came out. The secretary told him I was waiting to speak with him. Behind his closed office door, I explained I needed his signature to drop algebra.

"This is only the first day of class," he said. "Why don't you give yourself a chance?"

I insisted I had to drop.

"Why?" he said.

Then I told him what I had done, calling exponents the "little, tiny numbers." And I said I didn't want to waste any effort on algebra if it looked like I was too stupid to graduate.

There was no criticism of me, no condescension at all. He said, "I agree, you have to drop." After a somber moment, he reached for a stack of papers. Taking one off the top, he signed his name. I've often thought about how respectful Dean Burdine was. I left his office relieved, my infinitesimal self-esteem intact. I promised myself I would never knowingly make someone feel bad about his/her achievement, or lack thereof.

The rest of the classes went okay. The history professor was amazing. He stood at the podium in front of a huge Plan II class [about 150 students] and lectured without notes from the beginning, weaving a colorful tapestry of facts and stories. After a couple of weeks, he gave us an hour-long examination. Bringing the graded papers back to us with a frown on his face, he said, "Get out your pencils, put everything off your desk, and spell the following words." He dictated 100 words I knew how to spell.

The next class, he brought those spelling tests back to us, marked. I missed one: I couldn't remember whether it was *dietitian* or *dietician*. Mine was the highest score in the class. He spent about ten minutes excoriating the rest of the students on their poor spelling. He threatened them with a referral to the non-credit spelling lab. If a professor reported you to the spelling lab, you were required to go there until you learned to spell – You couldn't graduate without satisfying the spelling police. I was glad I didn't have to worry about remedial spelling.

From the first day, English class was over my head on topics I had never thought [or cared] about. Our first thousand-word essay, due the fifth week of class, was to write a comparison of Judaism as it is found in the Old Testament and Confucianism. I was sucked to the bottom of Biblical quicksand.

When he brought the papers back, he said, "Some of the papers were all right, none was excellent, and one student called the Jews in the Old Testament 'Christians.' Miss Crawford, may I see you in the hall?"

It was fourth grade all over again: the class was laughing at my Christian mistake as I followed Dr. Pratt out to the hall. He said, "I'd like to see your invitation to join Plan II."

Invitation? I had no invitation.

"Sorry. Would you repeat that?" I said.

"Did you receive an invitation to be in Plan II?"

I thought, *Obviously not!* Then I said, "No."

Face redder, voice louder, he said, "How did you get into the Plan II classes?"

Getting scared, I decided to throw a fictitious stranger under the bus rather than crawl under there myself.

"My sectionizer gave me the course card." This upset him further.

"Who was it?"

Of course, I couldn't tell him I was my own sectionizer, so I pleaded ignorance of how this mystery had occurred. "I don't know."

He demanded I describe the scoundrel; I said he was average height with brown hair. I'm sure he knew I was lying but couldn't prove it. He said he would remove me from the English class and let me join one of the regular classes. It turned out Plan II was for geniuses. I should have attended Orientation.

In the sixth week of classes, I belatedly joined a section of Freshman Comp for Dummies. When I got there, the class was writing an in-class essay with the title "Matriculation." Not sure of the meaning of matriculation myself, I rejoiced when another student asked about it.

"Registration," the professor explained. All I could think about was the trouble I'd been in recently with Plan II, and I had only an hour to write, so I wrote the sorry saga about deciding on an English major to escape the heat, continuing to the brouhaha of being removed from the smart Plan II class, pretty much as I've written it here.

The next class period, the professor stopped me in the hall and said, "Yours is the funniest essay I've ever received from a student. Good work!"

"Thanks," I said. "Don't tell Dr. Pratt." He laughed and assured me my secret was safe. At the end of the semester, I earned a C because I'd missed five weeks of the class.

Connor, these are memories I have of my education. I've done nothing to check their accuracy, so don't rely on my understanding.

The biggest and best surprise in my courses was German. The day I bought my text I saw the name *Deutsch I* in big letters on the cover for the first time. I was embarrassed to carry it because I didn't know what it meant. Later I discovered Germans called their language Deutsch. I was confused; why wouldn't they just call it German?

There was a language lab in Batts Hall, where recordings of German pronunciation led us through the initial stages of reading and speaking Deutsch. I didn't understand at first why this new language made so much sense to me. Then I found out English is a Germanic language. Who knew?

Anyway, it did make sense. There were not so many irregularities as in Latin. In fact, there weren't *any* irregularities I could see. German is easy to spell, no silent letters, a huge relief.

In German, as in English, the order of the words in the sentence carries much of the meaning, and they capitalize all the nouns. Most plurals end in /-en/, and participles begin with /ge-/ What could be easier?

Suffice it to say, I took to German like a duck takes to June bugs. I spent a lot of time on pronunciation in the lab. I'm sure I sounded nothing like a German, but in Texas I could get away with it.

At the end of the first semester, I made Cs in English, biology, and history, and a B in German. I thought about changing my major to Deutsch, since I learned I was good at it.

Real Trouble Begins

Sometime during my first year at UT, I lost my mind. After repeated arguments about my refusal, BF convinced me I ought to marry him. I couldn't give him a reason not to. I'd never learned "because I don't want to" is a good enough reason for anything, apart from death and taxes.

His "closer" was he would kill himself if I didn't marry him. Naïve to the point of insanity, I figured the least I could do was save his life. Justification: he was good in algebra, so he'd be a good provider. I had the verbal skills covered; his algebra would fill in one of the many blank spaces on the chart of my achievements. However, I failed to consider (a) I was not in love with him, and (b) he was boring as fog.

Case in point: Boyfriend had no narratives to add when my friends began to share. He loved our stories, but he contributed none of his own. For me, being good at algebra was enough; I thought I could entertain us alone. To be fair, I admitted his parents were Danish immigrants and knew no stories American teenagers would appreciate. They couldn't compete with Connie's murder of Eppie Marner or Sally's attempts to make me beautiful.

At the time, he looked deliriously happy. Fast forward several years, and he would have been better off if I'd told him to get lost. But I'm ahead of the story again.

My parents were delighted, and Mama started planning a June wedding. She wanted me to ask Fran to be matron of honor, but I refused. I couldn't tell her I hated my sister.

And what about my education? Daddy offered to pay for Boyfriend's tuition and expenses along with mine after we married because his parents were poor, and besides, he had made the dean's list with all his high grades. It was settled then. We would get an apartment in Austin in the fall and continue our courses of study in English and engineering. I decided not to change to a journalism major; I liked English!

Buoyed by a modicum of success in the first semester, in the spring I learned a little about how to study. My memorizing ability worked amazingly well. In history class, there wasn't a lot of difficult material to learn. It was just stories. So right after class I would return to my room and type my notes. After reading through them a few times, I found I had memorized enough of the content to get by. My strategy was to mark my notes with numbers and remember those, too. First this happened, then this, and on through the rest of the lecture.

Other students told me you didn't have to remember dates for history tests, but I couldn't "not remember." Whether it was a holdover from high school memorizing, my experience at the phone company, or whatever, my mind grasped numbers and wouldn't let them go. It was so bad I had to write down all the dates for the test when I first got the questions in order to relax while writing my essays. Writing them down cleared my mind to think.

My dream was to graduate from UT and to go to another part of the United States to teach in public schools. I was anxious to escape Carl, Galveston County, the acrid stench from oil refineries, life-threatening asthma, high heat, humidity, and a host of other horrors. I longed to see mountains, lakes, cities, forests, anything other than La Marque, Texas. Boyfriend agreed new horizons would be ideal. He would apply for jobs for mechanical engineers, accept the most advantageous for both of us, and we'd begin our professional lives.

In the meantime, life at UT went on. At the end of my freshman year, I married him. I admit I got a grave foreboding about the vows and their finality, but it happened two days before the wedding. When I told my mama I wasn't sure I wanted to get married, she exploded.

"Well, I'll be God damn! I sent out invitations, planned everything, and collected all these presents," she said, waving her arm toward the table groaning under sheets, china, and silver. "You WILL get married." So, Boyfriend became H, Husband. We shared my tiny college fund for both of us and went somewhat happily on our way.

Basic Movement

The 1957 UT catalog required all degrees four semesters of PT, physical training. Having exempted out of physical education in high school because of asthma, I had no idea what to expect. You could take some fun courses, like bowling or golf, but those required a sizeable fee to cover expenses. I had to take classes without a fee.

The UTPT requirements included passing a swimming test and Posture and Basic Movement, in which we students were in training for how to walk, sit at a desk, run, and climb the stairs. I could see no real value in these lessons because I had learned to walk, sit, run, and climb by age three. My pre-class posture grade was a B-, which kind of hurt my feelings.

Fortunately [or not] I had arranged to take this class with Connie. Each day we sat on the gym floor dressed in white shorts, shirts, and shoes, waiting for the professor to come show us how to walk, sit, run, and climb.

One morning I got to the gym early. Removing Connie's stuff from her locker, I put her shoes, shirt, shorts and socks in mine. I left a cryptic note saying "I got pig iron," reminiscent of "The Rock Island Line."

When I entered the gym, I found Connie dressed in her shorts, shirt, and tennis shoes. As I was trying to figure out what I had done wrong, the professor entered with a street-clothed student and said, "I have a note saying, 'I got gym clothes, gym shoes, and pig iron.' Does anyone know what this means?" It meant I had taken someone else's stuff and hidden it. I apologized, retrieved the girl's clothes, and no charges were filed.

My least favorite posture class was the day we climbed about ten flights of stairs. I complained so much Connie threatened me because she was afraid I would get her into trouble. The class dragged on until Christmas. My post-class posture grade was D-. I was insulted.

Having successfully demonstrated my walking, sitting, running, and climbing, I signed up for Modern Dance in the spring semester. The class met in the same building as Posture but in a different gym. There were several floors of four gyms each. The place was majestic.

Forget what you may have seen on other modern dance stages. We had no piano, props, costumes, or dignity. We were taught to run and jump in an artsy fashion. My running needed work because I ran like a girl, and the professor laughed when I jumped. I thought I could feel the building shake when I landed on my feet.

I hated Modern Dance. For one thing, not one of us had ever had a dance lesson. Dressed in our leotards, we writhed, twisted, crawled, and drifted across the gym floor, reminiscent of movie scenes of patients on the lockup floor of a psychiatric hospital. Without tights under my leotard, my skin didn't slide gracefully across the gym floor but developed a drag that occasionally squeaked.

The stretches and exercises getting us ready to run and jump made me so sore I could hardly walk. There were days I practically had to crawl up the stairs of the English Building. I was glad the posture professor couldn't see me. I cut Modern Dance so many times I was scared I'd fail it, but I guess few fail UTPT.

To graduate, UT students had to demonstrate their swimming prowess. Growing up, I didn't consider what I did swimming. Other people were freestyling, breathing air as they gracefully rolled to the side and turned their heads. I couldn't do it, but I could swim. Therefore, my sophomore year opened with a beginning swimming class. After one class period, I dropped. The objectives of the class were to pass the swimming test I had already passed.

We swimmers were assigned tank suits, which had big armholes and wide straps astride a rather low-cut bodice. They would have looked cute on twelve-year-old boys. However, my D-cup boobs immediately escaped to freedom out the sides. I could not keep myself covered. Even worse, every time I tried to do what the professor said, I sank to the bottom of the pool. "Form a circle, feet touching" sent me straight down. And forget raising one leg while floating on my back.

Afraid I would drown, I dropped and added badminton, another no-fee class. The sport was fraught with danger. One day my doubles partner decided to slam the shuttlecock down the throats of our rivals. Hitting it as hard as she could, she brought the racket straight to the bridge of my nose on her follow-through. I was left with a screaming headache, two black eyes, and permanent disfigurement.

My fourth and final semester of PT was tennis. Borrowing a racket from New Sally's friend in the Delta Gamma house, I did well on volleying, but I lacked enough coordination to toss the ball into the air and knock it across the net. Almost every time, it fell to the ground behind me, and I had to turn around and pick it up. The final exam was successful volleying and three proper serves. Praying for divine intervention, I managed to volley like a champ and squeak it over the net by a fraction of an inch the first three serves. For about ten minutes, I looked like a tennis player.

The Resident Across The Hall

Husband and I found an apartment a block from Memorial Stadium, presently the site of the LBJ Library. It was quite a walk to the English Building, located on the other side of the campus. The apartment had three rooms: a kitchen, living area, and bedroom, all on one side of a hallway. The furnishings were old but adequate. The kitchen stove was a green number straight out of the 1940s; the mattress on the bed had a spring poking through. The private bathroom was across the hall. H's favorite prank was to shout and jump at me when I exited the bathroom. He thought it was funny to give me a heart attack. Once after we saw "Psycho," he sneaked in and grabbed me through the shower curtain. I screamed and hit him in the face with a soapy washcloth, a knee-jerk reaction. He was offended.

One day in the spring of my junior year, I heard the car pull into the drive and stationed myself beside the stairs ready to jump at H. But it was the neighbor, Roger! When I yelled "Gotcha!" he dropped his pizza and books on the stairs. I apologized about ten times as I helped him retrieve his belongings, saying I was trying to teach my husband not to scare me. The remarkable thing is, he wasn't at all angry. In fact, after I scared him, he often stopped me in the hall to visit.

Like most married students, we were poor. $100 per month was really not enough for two to live on, even in the 1950s. Alternating tuna and peanut butter sandwiches, we studied most of the time and for entertainment attended ball games, concerts, and other freebies provided by the University. We also honed our contract bridge skills.

H's mother occasionally sent us the help-wanted ads from the *Houston Chronicle* in case I wanted to quit school and go to work to support us. My father detonated at the idea, so I didn't pursue it. I didn't want to go to work anyway. After a year at UT, I was already smart enough to know being a student is easier than working: fewer decisions! The professors told us what to read, what to write, how to read and write it, when to go to class and how to use the libraries. Work could possibly require difficult decisions on my part, and I didn't have a track record of making intelligent choices.

From Muleshoe, Texas, Roger was most unusual. Pretty much a loner, he talked mostly in a shout. I didn't see him often, but he was pleasant, and he'd chat with me. As it turned out, his mother knew my mother from years earlier. They were both from East Texas towns and had attended neighboring schools. Roger would sometimes stand in the hall and yell to me that his mother sent her regards to my family from Muleshoe.

His pants were unzipped. Then I noticed my mama couldn't take her eyes off his zipper. The two of them carried on a lengthy conversation, which I couldn't follow at all because I concentrated on her looking at him. When he went to his own apartment, I turned to face her.

"Mama," I said, "why were you staring at his zipper?"

"I was hypmatized!" she said.

THINGS START LOOKING BETTER

As a sophomore, I took a second American history class, a required course identified as flunk-out like English, biology, government, and the other required courses. Student rumors spread: the UT administration made freshman and sophomore courses extra hard. *To get rid of students like me*, I thought. I was never sure that my present semester wouldn't be my last.

A history hour-exam was coming up toward the end of the semester. I would have studied on my weekend trip, but I lacked enough discipline/focus to read and memorize four long chapters on a beautiful holiday I spent on the beach with my friends. Returning to Austin, a little sunburned, I was in a panic about the exam. At the appointed hour, I couldn't make myself attend class, but I needed a doctor's excuse to miss the test. It was a hot day, so I ran through the sunshine to elevate my temperature and entered the health center; my temperature registered 100 degrees. I made sure to get a doctor's note when I left. I canvassed other students about what the exam would likely be like. My take-away was they never asked about wars or presidential elections.

It was agreed I could take a make-up quiz at the end of the week. However, instead of four chapters, I would be responsible for the ten we had covered since the class began. I knew my situation was dire.

When I got the test questions in my hands, there were only two: Compare the Spanish American War with World War I, and trace the course of American politics through elections from Washington to Theodore Roosevelt. *Jesus, help me*. The two areas I had not studied at all!

I started to write what I could remember about the wars from a movie about yellow fever outbreaks during the early part of the twentieth century and the horrors of war in *A Farewell to Arms* by Ernest Hemingway. For the second essay, I couldn't remember much about the issues expressed during the American elections, but, thanks to Judy and my eleven-year-old self, I could trace the elections from Washington, through Tyler, Polk, Taylor, successfully through the Civil War, and all the way to Teddy Roosevelt. I sprinkled slogans I recalled from my reading: "Tippee canoe and Tyler, too," "24-40 or Fight," and "A chicken in every pot." When the prof returned the test to me, he had written, "A. An excellent example of thinking under pressure." He detected my B.S.

The zoology professor was uncharacteristically kind, unlike the many who taught freshmen and sophomores and couldn't be bothered with us. On the first lab practical exam I made 60 percent. I'd never taken a practical exam before and had not prepared correctly. The prof laid out about fifty items on tables; students formed a line and went around to each item to identify. We were given one minute to write the answer, then a bell rang, signaling advancement to the next item. I learned to memorize illustrations and diagrams in the text class and notes. I loved his longer tests, which were different from the others. On one exam, the first question read, "The _____ and _____ _____ _____ _____ to _____ a _____." I played with those blanks until I could fill them: "The egg and the sperm go together to form a zygote." I was the only one in the class to get it right, and we almost had a class mutiny. I never heard so much complaining about a question.

The botany professor was from Australia, speaking with the most wonderful accent. In one lecture, he said, "Dicotyledons have flowerpots of twos and their multiples." After he said *flowerpots* a few times, I raised my ignorant hand and asked him why the flowerpot made any difference in the kind of plant it contained. He looked at me closely, I guess to determine whether I was joking. Then he wrote on the board "P-A-R-T."

"Oh," I said, "PART!" I don't think he knew how much I liked him and his class.

In English classes, I could memorize long passages from poems and stories to illustrate my points in essay tests. Husband was in a different section of sophomore English. His professor assigned Juliet's balcony speech for the class to memorize. He went around the apartment for days saying it out loud. "Thou knowest the mask of night is on my face, else would a maiden blush bepaint my cheek..." I memorized it before he did and corrected him when he made a mistake or paused trying to remember.

After the first semester, I made a B average over five courses. I was beginning to get the hang of this UT stuff. I received a tuition scholarship each subsequent semester.

In our junior year, Connie and I took one more class together, American Literature from 1865 to the present. J.G. Varner was the professor. His focus was mainly on Edgar Allen Poe, but he took us through the second half of the nineteenth century and the first half of the twentieth. My tastes in poetry hadn't changed much since high school and the black pit in "Invictus."

Thomas Cranfill's course on Shakespeare crystallized my resonance for morbid poetry: "When in disgrace with fortune and men's eyes, I all alone beweep my downcast state." Exactly how I felt.

Depressed and a suicide wannabe, when I got to the University of Texas English Department, I was drawn to Edgar Allen Poe's stories and poems about loneliness and grief. I found a kinship in William Cullen Bryant, who, at sixteen, wrote "Thanatopsis," a kind of morality lesson about death. Here was my kind of teenager! *Everyone has to die*, he thought, *so do it well.*

So live, that when thy summons comes to join the innumerable caravan, which moves to that mysterious realm, where each shall take his chamber in the silent halls of death, thou go not like the quarry slave at night, scourged to his dungeon, but sustained and soothed by an unfaltering trust, approach thy grave like one who wraps the drapery of his couch around him and lies down to pleasant dreams.

Throughout this English major, we read depressing existential novels, such as Camus' *The Plague* and Steinbeck's *The Grapes of Wrath*. I could go on and on with other titles, all dark. But you get the idea. English classes had begun to prepare me for my own "silent halls of death."

In my sophomore philosophy class, I learned how loosey-goosey were my understanding and knowledge of myself and the world. We studied Plato, who said everything is a copy or shadow of its original concept. For example, my desk exists as an individual copy of the original ideal, the archetypal desk. In his allegory of the cave Plato illustrates his view of reality by viewing us as people sitting in a cave facing a wall. Behind us is a fire throwing onto the wall of the cave shadows of people and things between us and the fire. Thus, all we see are shadows of the real. The allegory of the cave made perfect sense to me: I learned nothing is real.

I had the same experience with the rest of the philosophers we studied: Descartes, Kant, and Sartre. With each new philosopher, I tossed out the previous one and adopted the most recent. Descarte's mantra was, "I think, therefore, I am." This made sense to me. I concluded I thought, and therefore I was.

Sartre was interesting. He said life is like waking up and finding yourself on a train racing through a black night. You don't know how you got on the train or where it is taking you. As you fight panic, trying to figure it out, you see the conductor making his way down the center aisle collecting tickets. And you don't have a ticket!

In his book *The Wall,* Sartre tells the story of a man who is in prison condemned to die for a crime he didn't commit. He works hard at understanding his situation and imminent death until he comes to accept them and even agrees with them. At the end, his sentence makes sense to him. Then suddenly, he learns his conviction has been overturned, and he is free to go. He refuses and insists his execution must be carried out because freedom is illogical.

By the end of the semester, I was totally nuts.

On occasion, I run into ideas reminiscent of Plato's allegory. When, for example, breaking sound and meaning into their minimal units in the study of descriptive linguistics, every single sound we utter or hear is an abstract representative of the ideal. Called *allophones*, no two sounds are the same, even when pronounced or heard by the same person. Thus, for example, there is one /t/ ideal; all the /t/ sounds spoken or heard are but representatives of it.

T.S. Elliott, in his poem "The Hollow Men," wrote, "Between the idea and the reality falls the shadow." How true. Not long ago I had the *idea* to bake a red velvet cake from scratch. In the mixing, I failed to include baking powder, the leavening ingredient. The *reality* turned out to be two red frisbees, flat and round, which I sailed over the back yard wall into the creek for the birds.

Senior Year

In my senior year I was hired as a grader in the English Department. I graded papers and kept the gradebook current, for three professors: the head of the department, a freshman composition professor, and Dr. Varner, my favorite English professor.

Dr. Varner and I spent some afternoons in his office discussing issues of the world, or more accurately, issues of the University of Texas at Austin. I ran my experiences past him, including people I had met, books I'd read, and my perspectives on life in general.

A pipe smoker, Dr. Varner put his pipe into his mouth, lit a match, and talked until the match burned down to his fingers. Then he tossed the match over his shoulder and started again. He told me about his research in Spain, how he read manuscripts of ancient monks, translating archaic Spanish into English. "The monks seldom lifted their pens from the parchment, so I had to supply breaks between the words." In return, I told him stories about my mother and other family members, my friends, and some of what I was learning from my courses at UT.

"You ought to be a writer," Dr. Varner said.

"I can't be a writer," I said, "because writers have to know something. I don't know anything."

"That's what I mean," he said, laughing.

I finally suffered through algebra in my senior year. When I went to see the professor each week for help, he repeatedly said they shouldn't require English majors to take the same algebra as engineers. I squeaked by only with a huge infusion of tutoring by both Husband and Professor Mills, a retired Navy captain. He sent us to the blackboard to work problems in front of the class.

Well, he sent the other students to the blackboard because he knew once he gave me a problem, he would spend the rest of the class trying to teach it to me. "This row, man the blackboards, except for Elizabeth."

At the end of the semester, in an almost daily visit to his office, I told him I informed my father I would probably receive a D in algebra and postpone graduation.

"I appreciate so much how hard you tried to teach it to me," I said. "I will take it again and be sure to get into your class next semester." I recognized years later my extortion of a C from a kind, generous person. It had not been my intent. Since graduation I have proven (a) you can be well educated, and (b) live a full life without knowing algebra.

During the three years between my wedding and graduation, I was optimistic about my future. I knew, while I wasn't Plan II material, I was smart enough to get an English degree. When I thought about where we would go and what we would do in the future, I hoped we could go other places to live. When I imagined weekends exploring other cities or towns, Husband agreed: new frontiers sounded good to him, too. I was especially hoping for the Pacific Northwest, where the climate was cooler and the air cleaner than in Southeast Texas. I fantasized about sightseeing in the mountains, where geography and local history, so different from the Texas Gulf Coast, were full of new and exciting adventures.

I graduated a year before H, whose degree required more semester hours than mine. To await his graduation, I accepted a teaching position back on the Gulf Coast, where I could stay with my parents to save money for a year. The year I spent without him was happy, but not necessarily happier than the years we'd lived together in Austin. There was something about Austin promising excitement and hope for new horizons.

WORK

Mentally tucking my lifetime Texas [English] teaching certificate under my arm, age twenty-one, I began the new school year in Dickinson, just a short distance from La Marque. Our plan was to live with my parents while H finished his engineering degree. Upon his graduation, we would leave the Gulf of Mexico for *la dolce vita*.

In 1961, schools were not air-conditioned. My first teaching assignment was seventh grade accelerated English, eighth-grade reading, and ninth-grade English. We'd had class for a week when we learned there was a storm in the Gulf. Deadly still, the air hung around and on us like drapes. The oppressive heat drained us, students and teachers alike. At the end of the day, I went home and went to bed. Then Hurricane Carla struck Galveston head on, dead center. Schools were closed, the buildings used as shelters for people in low-lying areas.

My parents stayed in Kemah, where they owned a pharmacy on the shore of Galveston Bay. H and I stayed in La Marque in their home, about twenty miles south. When the weather people predicted a twelve-foot storm surge, it was clear the store would be inundated. Although we were much closer to Galveston, they were in greater peril because of the Bay. At 10:00 P.M., as Hurricane Carla sat offshore increasing intensity, Daddy called us to come to Kemah.

"Bring boxes, bags, anything you can find to pack out the store."

In the hour's drive to reach them, the south wind rocked the car as we dodged flying debris through sheets of rain on the dark road. We hoped we could clear the pharmacy before the bay washed over us. The four of us worked into the night, shoving merchandise into trash bags and boxes. Daddy cleared the shelves of prescription drugs, recording the contents of each box. We made several trips in our cars to the Dickinson Pines, some twenty miles away, to deliver our stash to Dee Cryar's home.

At dawn, the job was complete. Then we went to Dickinson to ride out the storm, pharmacy stock stacked to the ceiling in Dee's dining room. And we waited. Initially, we were glad the storm didn't move over Galveston right away. The delay gave us time to salvage what we could in a building not insured against rising water. But two days went by and still the storm sat offshore, getting stronger, growing into a Category 5 hurricane. Finally on the third day, it started to push toward us. As the wind grew stronger around us, we could hear the staccato snaps of pine trees around the house.

The neighborhood lost power early on. We couldn't open windows because of the rain and wind. A door to a covered patio afforded little ventilation in the stifling atmosphere. Radio reports of tornadoes in Galveston terrified us. We sat in the hot, dark house and awaited the worst.

At the storm's loudest, pine trees crashing to the ground around the house, our hostess took her children to a back bedroom; I went with them. We kneeled in a circle on the carpet and said the rosary. Well, *they* said the rosary; I was Methodist, but I acted like a Catholic. The Rosary offered a comforting feeling, as though we were taking action to make the hurricane more survivable. As the saying goes, "any port in a storm."

On the fourth day, the eye of the storm passed over us. The quiet outside was eerie, but we were relieved. After almost an hour, the wind started again, this time from the north. It was almost over.

Wind whistling around us, we made our way over to Kemah, where we found the store with seven feet of water inside. The back wall of the building had blown away, which was a good thing. The store was insured against wind damage.

When school started a week after Hurricane Carla, I was faced with a huge learning curve. The [junior high] students were anxious and restless because of the storm, and I didn't know how to calm them down. I didn't have clear routines for making up work, late work, no work. I had no idea how to teach English. I could teach poetry and prose appreciation, but my students couldn't read the poems and stories. And how do you teach anyone to write? I felt inadequate.

For one thing, we taught seventh grade spelling by rules. You know, "I before e, except after c, or as vowels pronounced /-ay/, as in neighbor and weigh." As I was teaching the rule, I thought of seize. Rules don't always work.

I learned the rules along with the students until we got toward the end of the book when they became incomprehensible. There was one I couldn't wrap my mind around until the seventh graders taught it to me:

> If there is a two-syllable word with the accent on the second syllable, ending in a final consonant preceded by a single vowel, double the final consonant when adding a suffix beginning with a vowel. [For example, *occur | occurring*, and *compel | compelled*.]

Accelerated seventh graders had studied those rules several years and understood them well. But what of the uninitiated, like me? To many the rules made no sense.

I assumed people in junior high school could read, but I found out not always. Children who "missed it" in elementary school were out of luck with secondary English teachers, whose preparation to teach concentrated on the split between grammar and literature. There was no preparation for teaching older students word recognition, vocabulary acquisition, literal and interpretive meanings of text, main ideas and supporting details, making predictions, drawing conclusions, and other salient reading skills. My education classes had dealt with educational psychology, philosophy of education, and other general subjects.

I read all the education books on teaching reading I could find. The trouble was, they were designed for primary level. In my attempts to find age-appropriate materials to use as texts, I had to replace bunny rabbits with sports figures. I abandoned phonics – the sound-it-out method – which was perceived by teens as insulting.

As I learned years later in my doctoral studies, phonics isn't as effective with older students, who stop concentrating on sounds and look more at meanings. The researcher, Uta Frith, theorized three stages of learning to read: beginning readers look at shapes of words and associate their meanings. Think <u>STOP</u> for the traffic sign and <u>Fruit Loops</u> for cereal. The next step is the sound-it-out phase, in which students learn the alphabet and many of the corresponding sounds of each letter. In the final stage of learning to read, students will recognize word parts from repeated exposure and match them to their own internal dictionary. For this reason, it makes sense to teach word recognition through sight words and word families, like <u>ran</u>, <u>can</u>, <u>fan</u>; <u>mor</u> [<u>amorous</u>], <u>path</u> [<u>sympathy</u>], and <u>lum</u> [<u>illuminate</u>, <u>luminous</u>].

I began to drink alcohol during the first year of teaching, mostly beer. On weekends I would drink with friends I worked with; when H was home on weekends, we all drank beer together, and we played a lot of contract bridge.

As the school year drew to a close, H's opportunities opened. He interviewed for jobs at Boeing in Seattle, Schlumberger in Louisiana, and NASA in Houston. He accepted Schlumberger, known for its oil/gas exploration. I was eager to move to rural Louisiana, excited about exploring antebellum plantations, Cajun culture, zydeco, and fresh seafood.

However, about a month after signing with Louisiana, H soared into outer space, switching jobs to the National Aeronautics and Space Administration located in South Houston.

I was devastated. I can't describe the despair I felt. His was a unilateral decision that did not include me. I wanted to leave Galveston County behind, but I was back for good.

A couple of years later, NASA moved to its permanent headquarters in Webster, about fifteen miles from where I'd grown up. My life lost its sunshine. I felt the only hope for me was somehow to get him to change his mind. He refused, citing the good salary, job security, and outstanding retirement package offered by NASA. I was twenty-four and not ready to retire; I had a lot of exploring left in me, but I didn't know the concept of deal-breaker.

I was imprisoned. I cried, prayed, and drank too much, trying to forget my dream. It didn't work. H loved working at NASA on the space capsule's heat shield team. Meanwhile I taught junior high English and reading. For a while I could get relief from my unhappiness by concentrating on my students; however, the hard, hot work of teaching wore on me. After a year of teaching, a shroud of depression settled over me, obscuring everything good about my life.

KISS

After six years of marriage, I became pregnant. I thought I was a victim of life itself. My days were the result of decisions made by others. I don't know when I gave up fighting, but sometime during those early years, I tried to do what was expected of me by principals, parents, Husband, and everyone else.

I took a year off from teaching and spent nine months in bed crying. As soon as he left for work, deep, aching sobs started, and they didn't stop until right before he came home. It took all my strength to get up, wash my face, and straighten the house. It didn't occur to me to talk to anyone else about my unhappiness. I thought you had to be strong and play the cards you were given in this life, not complain about being unhappy. I told myself, "Well, ya damn fool, you shouldn't have married him."

When Kiss was seven months old, I went back to work, hoping to ease my unhappiness, but the pit grew blacker and deeper. I found a job in Hitchcock teaching ninth-grade English. The change of school districts kept me busy. I was glad to have ninth grade because I could get by with one major preparation for classes. However, the principal threw me a curve by scheduling for me one class of physical education.

"You have got to be kidding me," I said. He couldn't or wouldn't change my assignment, so I was stuck with PE for an hour every day. My students had an academic year in dodgeball. I didn't know what else to do.

In the afternoon I drove back home and picked up Kiss. Then I busied myself cooking dinner and doing laundry. Weekends saw a mountain of ironing. It's difficult for me to believe I cleaned the house, did the entire laundry, and ironed H's starched white shirts with no help at all. I tried to make it effortless, but there was no way washing clothes and ironing a week's laundry was not a big deal. H came home each day and read the newspaper while I cooked dinner. I resented it! And I hated him! However, it never occurred to me to refuse.

The only bright spots in my day were the times I played with Kiss. What can you say about a child who gave you a reason to carry on, to live one day at a time? She and I sang songs, among them a drinking song of the time called "Those were the days." I taught her to belt it out with all the gusto she could muster at three.

About this time, H decided to enroll in flying lessons. A good thing from my perspective. I knew I was smart enough to support myself and child; therefore, I thought the way out for me was widowhood. My fantasy changed from suicide to flying accident. I became obsessed. I had a scenario playing in my mind: *two FBI agents ring my doorbell with the [un]happy news of H's demise. Can I avoid showing my joy?*

After several months of safe flying on his part, I tried to figure out how I could kill him without jeopardizing myself. I didn't want to go to prison. I felt like a shattering mirror; only fragments of me retained an image. Fortunately, a rare moment of clarity invaded my consciousness in the form of a voice in my head saying, "Look what you've become." If Jesus were right and the thought is as bad as the deed, I had become a murderer. I had gone from hating myself to hating H. I had turned into a psychic cesspool, and I was careful to tell no one.

I suffered a breakdown, crying nonstop sometimes for hours, but successfully hiding it. I would go into the restroom in the teacher's lounge between classes and cry. There is a scene in the film *Mrs. Dalloway* in which she goes into the bathroom to cry, trying to fake a cheerful voice through the door. Hidden tears were years seven to eleven of my marriage to H. Suicide once again looked better than life.

The first year of desegregation in Hitchcock schools was in 1965, and I was glad I was teaching ninth grade. Freshmen were not as eager to fight as seniors, and I had learned a modicum of strategies to survive in the classroom. I realized I had come full circle to the Hitchcock of my childhood. Where was my progress?

My classes were well mannered, but there was one boy who talked so much the students around him complained they couldn't hear the lessons. Joseph was a big, burly kid who had the maddening habit of repeating everything people said. I learned later this was called echolalia, a bona fide disorder; at the time, however, I called it disrespectful. I moved him to the front of the room to give students at the back a break from his chatter. Then he repeated everything I said.

On a day I had ironically written my own name on the absentee list by mistake, Joseph was especially active. Dressed in a white tee shirt and jeans, he looked like he didn't know he was doing anything wrong. Each time I warned him to be quiet, he quietly ignored me and began repeating my words as soon as I resumed speaking.

I stood at the front of the room pointing at the blackboard with my ruler, a heavy wooden one with a metal strip down the side. Joseph was at his best, happily repeating the lesson on possessive nouns and pronouns.

"Will you shut up?" I said.

"Control yourself," Joseph said, quoting an Anacin commercial. "Sure, you're tense and irritable, but don't take it out on the children."

My knee-jerk reaction was to bring the ruler, metal strip first, down hard on his forehead, perpendicular to his hair line, right between his eyes. He stopped talking as his eyes teared. I know I hurt him. There was no sound in the classroom as the other students waited to see what was next. I walked out into the hall to calm down. After a minute or two I reentered the room and continued the lesson.

After I hit him, Joseph's repetitions were a thing of the past, never again to distract me or anyone else in the class. As far as I know, no one outside of my classroom ever knew what happened. To my relief, I never heard from a parent, principal, or the NAACP about it. I had discovered a cure for echolalia.

Levi Fry

In the spring of 1966, the principal of Levi Fry Junior High in Texas City recruited me to teach ninth-grade English.

"I heard you can teach older students to read," he said. He offered me a bigger salary and a good opportunity to escape teaching physical education. I jumped at it.

I requested the bottom 100 ninth-grade achievers. My offer to the principal was to take the lowest scoring students in the ninth grade if I had no more than twenty students in a class. He agreed. The early 1960s were the days before special education, before mainstreaming, before students became surly and disrespectful.

Ninth-grade English required the study of a novel. In the bookroom, old copies of mostly boring books provided classroom sets of classics written by dead white guys, titles found in what is called the canon, the traditional curriculum. Students who hate to read could get their best sleep in the time it takes to read a book like *Silas Marner*. Unable to find a title I could get excited about, I went to the principal with a request for twenty-five copies of *Mutiny on the Bounty*, figuring teenage boys would likely find 19th century seafaring conflict exciting.

I was sure swashbuckling would be to the boys' liking. While *Mutiny* was classified as fiction, the boys liked that it was based on a true story – I found boys usually prefer nonfiction to fiction. Girls are usually happy just with a good story. All were sad to finish reading the book. When I told them there were two more novels revealing what happened to Captain Bligh and the mutineers, they wanted to read those, too. The principal was pleased and provided the books.

Next came Shakespeare, another requirement. Instead of the maudlin *Romeo and Juliet*, I chose *Midsummer Night's Dream* because of its frolicking good time. There's a play within the play, created by a few unpoetic poets. The character's names are funny, and the things they say are hilarious. The humor is worth wading through Elizabethan English. In the end, Puck, a sprite, observes, "Lord, what fools these mortals be." The students laughed their way through Shakespeare.

In American education in the 1960s, there was a surge of government spending on strategies for increasing students' reading ability, and the monies for reading instruction were abundant. Unfortunately, of the new materials, not all the purchases were well chosen. Case in point, the tachistoscope – a machine designed during WWII to help plane spotters more quickly identify planes overhead. The justification for the speed builder was time saved between spotters' identification of enemy aircraft and instant recognition. The tachistoscope projected pictures of American, German, and Japanese planes to facilitate faster visual perception.

Without much research on the tachistoscope's influence on reading instruction, it was offered to schools on the theory that improving speed of perception would increase readers' acuity. Most teachers didn't want to mess with it, but I decided to give it a go. After familiarizing myself with the tachistoscope's operation, I chose a program of five-digit numbers in varying speeds. Set at one-tenth of a second, the tachistoscope projects the image on the screen. If you blink, you lose it! Alerting students to pay attention, I instructed them to concentrate on the numbers, "Take a picture in your brain." They were not to say anything before they wrote the numbers on their paper. It went something like, "Look," then "Write." The sequence of five digits went dark in one-tenth of a second.

"Shit." Usually a quiet, shy girl, Sherry, signaled her dismay. Along with everyone else, she missed it. I pretended I didn't hear her. As time went on, students were able to see they could do something at the end of the class they couldn't do at the beginning. We increased the number of digits to seven over time. I discovered the tachistoscope served to "wake up" the students and increase their concentration, enabling them to be more alert to printed material.

If a new student arrived at the school destined for my English class, I would transfer the highest-achieving student to another teacher to maintain my class load of twenty. One day in late spring, a boy joined us – with an attitude. He took some time to settle into a desk toward the back of the room and then proceeded to heckle me, much as drunks interrupt stand-up comedians. I was about to address the problem when Cecil got up and walked back to the newcomer's desk. Before I could prevent it, Cecil balled his fist and slugged the boy in the middle of the chest.

"Don't make her mad," he said. "If she gets mad, we'll have to do some damn vocabulary!"

One Saturday night in May, I received a telephone call from Cecil at 3:00 A.M.

"Come get me; I'm in jail."

"Cecil, it's 3:00 A.M. Call your mother."

"I can't," he said. "I only get one phone call."

"Give me her phone number and I'll call her," I said. He did, and I did.

My daily routine during this time was to take Kiss to the babysitter, drive the forty-five minutes to Fry Junior High, teach all day, retrieve Kiss on my way home, fix dinner, do laundry, and then go to bed. When she was a baby, Kiss had colic and didn't sleep all night. We were both sleep-deprived and worn out. Some nights I held her and walked the floor, my tears falling on her baby blanket.

Master's Degree

More than ever before, I wanted to get away, away from the polluted air around the oil refineries; away from rice and other crops creating pollen-induced asthma; and away from all contact with my sister and her husband. I stopped teaching after six years and accepted a marketing position with American Education Publications, publishers of *My Weekly Reader*. Life was less painful on the road. I traveled throughout the South and Southwest, marketing seven different classroom newspapers.

At home I felt like a hostage. I had married "till death do us part." But he wouldn't die, and I was afraid to help him along with dying because of a thousand reasons. So, I just kept working as the *Weekly Reader* lady. Being on the road in a job is lonely; I longed to be with my toddler. I was going to have to get a divorce before I did something to ruin all our lives.

I divorced H when Kiss was four. We fought for custody. I won. I went back into the classroom at Alvin Junior College teaching reading and writing to disadvantaged students. I wasn't being paid enough to support us, so I looked around for other opportunities. I found a notice of a doctoral program in junior college reading in Las Cruces, New Mexico. I didn't even have a master's but applied anyway.

When Kiss was five, she shared with my mother that Fran's husband, the brother of my abuser, was exposing himself to her. She said he told her no one would believe her if she told, but she didn't care. My mother believed her, and when she told me, I believed her, too. At that point I made a decision to leave Texas.

I went back into classroom teaching, this time at a junior college as a Title I reading teacher.

The new federal funding offered opportunities for reading instruction to adults. To get this money, colleges set up language labs for adults who had not learned to read well. I think I was the second Texan hired to design a reading instruction program for adults. My students were mostly women from inner-city Houston who wanted to train to become nurses. The dean of the college wanted me to teach speed reading, which makes little sense. What good is teaching speed to people who don't understand written text? You're simply teaching them to misunderstand faster. I learned to disguise my basic reading instruction as speed reading. The other professors blamed me because their students couldn't read. If I tried to teach the desperate women some skills necessary for writing an essay, the English teachers made me desist. I was supposed to teach speed reading only.

To qualify for teaching at the post-secondary level – to do what I was doing – I needed a master's degree. I applied for a new junior-college reading education degree at the graduate school at New Mexico State University in Las Cruces. Packing for a major change, my little girl and I left Southeast Texas and moved to the Land of Enchantment where I was accepted into a doctoral program in junior college reading. However, because I had no master's degree, the University offered me a master's degree for the Ph.D. coursework. There were eleven other students in the program, all working on their doctorates. Sometimes they looked to me for a reality check because I was the only one in the class who had taught junior college reading.

Las Cruces was a desert city largely made of adobe buildings. New Mexico State, a huge university, maintained a number of two-bedroom cement-block houses for married students. My little girl and I moved into one of those only a block from the Education Building. She joined me after I moved all our belongings west.

I loved living in this new place and being free. Kiss and I explored mountains, little towns, and El Paso on weekends. During the week in the summer, she went to class with me, taking along her coloring book, crayons, and soft drink. She played outside with neighborhood children in the afternoons. She started first grade in a neighborhood school in August.

However, all the good things about my time in Las Cruces could not compensate for the drinking making my life increasingly unmanageable. I switched from beer to brandy, a lot of brandy. After Kiss went to bed, I drank more than ever. I tried to slow my descent into alcoholism, but I didn't want to quit drinking. I just wanted to stop drinking so much. I promised myself only one drink, but the first drink turned into a river. Nursing headaches and nausea some mornings, I had to act like I felt better than I did.

A part-time job as graduate assistant – typing, stapling, grading papers and conducting informal reading tests in the local elementary school for my boss' research – earned enough money to see me through. My classes were going very well. The years of teaching English to high school students had given me a modicum of confidence in my writing ability, and my junior college reading experience had prepared me for this master's program. My course grades depended on research papers in the various classes. There were no examinations, and happily, there was no mathematics!

Connor, this part of my story is painful to remember. I didn't act like a loving wife and mother through my eleven-year marriage, and my behavior in New Mexico was worse. I had been so unhappy most of my life. When freedom finally came for me, I didn't know what to do. I just went wild.

There was a man in my master's class I admired. I thought he was wonderful. We married after ten days of being together. After the wedding, after the first day of the marriage, we slipped and slid downhill. I drank more, causing ever more problems, but Husband[2] was the love of my life.

The Mexican Border

I admit my second marriage was not one of my best decisions. H^2 was studying for a doctorate and I for a master's degree in junior college reading programs. Like moths and fire, we collided almost immediately. After a month of dating, our marriage began on our best day and spiraled down in flames for the next eight years, like airplanes in World War II movies. We drank a lot of alcohol to pretend we were happy.

Las Cruces, New Mexico, lies just 45 miles from the Mexican border if you go through El Paso. In 1971, we were new to New Mexico State University and eager to explore the Chihuahuan Desert, chili-pepper food, and each other. My 30-year-old psyche was hungry for adventure. A trip across the border to buy groceries provided my self-image with an exaggerated sense of cosmopolitan worldliness.

Border Patrol guards with huge dogs questioned people coming out of Mexico as we were driving in. Anxiety seized me in our first trip down the dusty Mexican street in our old Plymouth station wagon, a yellow behemoth we called the banana. As I gazed out the window, H^2 said, "Mexican authorities consider an automobile accident a felony offense, punishable by jail or prison."

I watched cars and scooters speed in every direction, dodging each other, tourists on foot, and tiny children sidestepping cars. Sidewalk and street teemed with beggars and barkers vying for attention in hopes of gaining American currency. Horns honked and people shouted. Dogs barked. Jesus, help us all.

At first, I worried about the safety of foreign food, but in shopping, I found wonderful cookies, fruits, snacks, and crackers. I tasted delicious baked goods with Mexican not-soprocessed sugar which lacked the cloying "bite" of ours. Fruits were colorful and plump, and crisp chips tasted of chili powder and lime. A full bar occupied the center aisle of the supermarket, and a dance floor lay off to the left in front of a bandstand where a couple of trumpet players joined a few guitars in loud strains—and I use that word advisedly—of "La Paloma." I avoided the counter of plucked ducks and chickens hanging aloft by their necks. H² and I added two liters of Anejo rum to our purchases and returned to the banana.

When I confided in him my fear of authorities in uniform, he said, "Nothing to worry about. When we get to the border guards, they will ask you one question: 'Citizenship?' All you have to say is 'U.S.', and I will handle everything else."

At the border behind about a dozen cars, I dreaded the official encounter with every move up the queue. To quiet my fears, I practiced my line, "U.S.," and read all the signs listing things you can't bring into the U.S.:

- More than two liters of alcohol per month
- Guns
- Ammunition
- Controlled substances
- Medications, except for personal use – with a doctor's prescription

Well, Connor, when we reached the guard, H² lowered his window.

"Citizenship?" Check.

"U.S.?" Check.

"Go to Gate 7 to pay the import fee," the guard said.

H² accelerated right past Gate 7, insisting that Texas had no right to charge tariffs. A Californian, he didn't know authorities reign supreme in Texas. Terrified, I watched behind us to be sure they weren't coming after us.

***

H² and I continued our weekend forays into Juarez. After a couple of weeks, he found a hole-in-the-wall food counter that specialized in what they called the Fred Sandwich. Assuring me it was safe to eat, he ordered two. After a short time, I held in my hand a soft, chewy bun filled with slices of ham, cheese, and crisp lettuce. Instead of mayonnaise, a mild guacamole graced the bread. Ignoring warning signs to the contrary, I ate the sandwich, somewhat anxious about any afterlife it might have. *Delicioso*!

Since no *turista* trots kicked in, I turned my attention to the supermarket. Each week we bought more and more outstanding food. On that first Fred-sandwich day, I was surprised to read a notice that, because of some fungus or other, oranges were on the no-no list. However, we legally substituted tangerines. We bought our two liters of rum, returned to the banana and fled past Gate 7 like it wasn't even there. I was getting more comfortable with my Butch-Cassidy persona, but all comfort dissolved when H² turned right onto the highway instead of left toward Las Cruces.

"Where are we going?"

"You'll see," he said.

A mile later he turned right again, headed back to the border. A nauseating fear gripped me. He explained that we could walk across the border and get two more liters of rum.

What? Wait!

"It's simple," he said. "They don't know we drove across."

By *they*, I assumed he meant the Border Patrol, the people I was most scared of! Oh, Jesus! Here we go again. We crossed the border on foot. All went well until we got in line to cross back into Texas. There were two lines. The other people had the same routine as we did, but different guards. I noticed a woman in that line with about a dozen leather purses hanging around her neck. Interested, I neglected to practice my line, trying to figure out why she had all those heavy-looking bags hanging round her neck.

When she got to her officer, he said, "Citizenship?"

The woman said, "Ju ess."

Unconvinced, the guard said, "How long have you been a U.S. citizen?"

She answered, "I been a ju ess citizen a short distance."

Just as I was about to laugh, H^2 punched me to turn around and pay attention. The Border Patrol officer said, "Citizenship?"

"UUUhhhhh," I stammered, surprised.

"How many times have you crossed the border?" asked the guard.

"UUUhhhh." I hadn't practiced anything for this turn of events. I couldn't tell him innumerable times.

"We never have," H^2 said.

"Never?"

"Never!"

I stayed quiet and have little memory of getting out of that predicament alive. Had the guard asked to see it, my New Mexico driver's license would alert anybody with a brain that I was lying. We stayed legal for a couple of weekends, bringing only two liters per trip. Not legally legal, exactly, because we were allowed only two liters per month, but more legal than usual.

About a month later, as I admired the fruit in the Mexican supermarket, I spotted a sign indicating that this week's mangoes were not permitted in Texas. They were some of the biggest I had ever seen, yellow and pink and plump.

"Ooohh, Richard," I gushed. "Look at these mangoes. It's too bad we can't get them. They are beautiful."

"Get some," he said.

"They aren't allowed." Oh, foolish person. Of course he didn't listen to me.

"We'll put them in the bottom of the bag. No one will know."

Really? I thought, remembering the police dogs at the border. What if they were trained to sniff out mangoes as well as drugs? Nauseated with fear, I carried my contraband to the banana and started to practice saying "*U.S.*" with a sincere prayer to Jesus for mercy.

As we made our way up the long line to the border, anxiety paralyzed me. This time the officer was on the passenger side of the car. My side! I rolled down my window, and as he looked into the car, he made eye contact with me.

He said, "Got any mangoes in your car?"

"UUUhhh."

"No mangoes," H² said. At the guard's nod, we proceeded to bypass Gate 7 and made our way back to Las Cruces.

***

There were times we took Kiss across the border with us to get Fred Sandwiches and buy groceries. At six, she was as interested as I was in the differences between shopping in Mexico and in Texas. She wanted to go down all the aisles to look at the exotic offerings. She marveled at the toy aisle. There was no toy aisle in our Safeway! In the meat department, she stood open-mouthed, staring at plucked chickens and geese hanging by their necks above the refrigerated counter. I had to pull her away.

Once again in the banana, we took Kiss for a ride through Juarez, where we got hopelessly lost and couldn't find our way back to the border. Everything was different. Many homes were painted bright colors, greens and oranges. Most houses were fenced with formidable gates leading to open garages. Roofs were flat; some had wire fences around the roofs and Doberman pincers keeping guard up there.

The three of us were quiet during this trip of discovery. It's not surprising that we lost the border. At every turn there was more to see. We dodged handcarts and their owners selling frozen fruit juice on a stick. Dogs roamed freely in streets and alleys. We decided to turn back, but we got deeper and deeper into Juarez. Giving up on finding the border ourselves, H² stopped in front of a man selling ice cream.

"Ask him where the border is," he said to me.

"Ask him where the border is?" I repeated. "I don't speak Spanish."

H² reached down into his Berkeley degree in South American history and pulled out the question. He told me the words and said I could say it better than he could because I was from Texas.

I put my accent on the question, and the man told me in Spanish how to get to the border. I understood none of it, but thanked him and we sped off. Soon we were back in familiar territory.

We stopped at a restaurant three blocks from the bridge for paella. One of the waiters came to our table carrying a leather wineskin. He motioned to Kiss to watch his trick. He trained a stream of red wine from his forehead around his face to his mouth. Several times he performed the act, the wine making different paths through and around his features to his mouth. Kiss was freaked out. When she started crying, he left our table.

Back at the border, the officer asked, "Got any fruit?"

H² said *no*, but Kiss said, "What about the bananas?"

"Ssshhh," he said.

The guard smiled at her and winked. "Bananas are okay."

California

The year was 1972. I finished my Master of Arts in Teaching, and H² gave up on his doctorate that summer. It was, he said, time to go to work. We applied for teaching jobs across the West: California, Nevada, and Oregon. He was hired first, at Columbia Junior College in Sonora, California, up in the foothills of the Sierra Mountains, right in the heart of the "gold country."

Our first home wasn't a home at all, but a ski cabin high in the Sierras in a small community called Twain Harte. It was rustic beyond belief and furnished with the usual trash you put in cabins. The beds were hard and lumpy, the kitchen poorly equipped, and the water pipes prone to freeze. H² rented it without consulting me, and I hated it.

Having lived most of my life in warm Texas climes, most recently the New Mexican desert, I could not get warm. It was freezing! And this was August! Even on warm days, I had to stay in bed until noon when I could get up, wrap up, and start up my day. Doing what? you ask. Not much more than reading. We had a huge Franklin stove that warmed the whole cabin, but we didn't have enough wood. Each morning, I slipped out to the neighbor's house and stole a few sticks. Well? He had a big pile of wood!

Kiss enrolled in the local school, but after three months, I prevailed, and we moved down into the warmer central valley, to a little town called Oakdale, where we got a beautiful apartment in whiffing distance of the Hershey's factory. I think I gained weight just smelling their product. Again, Kiss enrolled in the local school, but about three months later, H² found a "better" town closer to his college.

Connor, this is painful for me to write because we jerked Kiss out of one school after another. We lived in Valley Springs, next, and I found a ninth-grade English position in Calaveras High School. There were only five English classes in the ninth grade, and my plan was to teach the students to write, beginning with the sentence and paragraph level.

The other teachers were sad to see me leave the following year when, once again, we uprooted Kiss to move to Sacramento where H² established a reading lab at another junior college. I signed on at California State University Sacramento (CSUS) to bring probationary students up to freshman-level academic achievement in the verbal skills, reading and writing. It never occurred to me to refuse to move. I cried as I packed dishes and put them into a box. I felt I had married a gypsy.

I could tell I was veering away from myself and goals I had set, but I was powerless to change. As it happened, professional success came in the middle of abject personal failure. I was the academic "arm" of the Equal Opportunity Program (EOP) at CSUS, responsible for the tutoring center, where about a dozen student tutors were on hand to provide one-on-one instruction to help students in EOP and anyone else having difficulty with coursework.

One of the best features of the center was its inclusion of tutors from other disciplines. The Economics Department provided student tutors as did Mathematics. The French tutor was from Fiji. There was no stigma attached because there was nothing to suggest we were a special program for probationary students. Any student having difficulty could apply for a tutor; if we didn't have one, we found one.

At the beginning of the semester, I instructed the reading tutors to give informal reading inventories, which I wrote and evaluated. I could look at the kind of mistakes a student made and prescribe tutorial material. If you know what kind of mistake a student makes, you don't have to teach the whole reading curriculum. At the end of the academic year, many of the students scored college-level word recognition.

Teaching students to think is more difficult. I asked them if they ever read a textbook chapter but had no memory of it, and if they could consider it reading if they couldn't make sense of it. The best way I found to teach the thinking required was an oral "think aloud." If the student didn't get the information, the tutor would read and demonstrate the thinking required to decipher the text.

On weekends, my little family explored mining towns that hadn't yet become touristy. There was usually an old-timey hotel with a bar on the first floor. Watch the TV show "Bonanza" and you'll get the picture. A swinging door led inside, and you could stand at an ornate mahogany bar that was over a hundred years old. Behind the well-stocked bar, a huge mirror reflected shelves of beer mugs and glasses.

Occasionally, H^2 drove us high into the mountains, where we saw summer snow for the first time. The interstate skirted a stream bringing melted snow from the highest point to the valley's lakes and rivers. In Texas, land fronting roads and beaches are private property with signs warning everyone to keep out.

H^2 found unmapped roads across the mountains, logging trails, where our little Toyota coupe climbed to ridiculous heights above the valleys below. On one of these jaunts, terrified, Kiss and I held each other and looked out the car window down into the valley. We saw a car that had gone off the side of the road, its front tires hanging onto the trail by their fingernails, its back bumper resting warily on a straggly tree growing out of the side of the cliff. The occupants of the car stood around, peering over the edge. Another car had stopped to help them, so we continued on up the mountain. H^2 never got scared, but Kiss and I said prayers and put pillows around our heads a lot of times.

"In California," he said, "it's all public land." Sightseers climbed on the rocks in the cold-water streams and picnicked in meadows and wonderful forests throughout Northern California. Not a posted sign in sight. Along the lesser roads, we found pomegranate and fig trees heavy with fruit. In the yard of one of our temporary bivouacs, Mountain Ranch in Calaveras County, stood a walnut and an almond tree. We attended the Jumping Frog Festival in Angel's Camp each June where Kiss chose a frog from a huge tank, took it onto the stage, and raced it against others. I don't remember that hers ever won.

We lived in an apartment in Sacramento a few months – another school for Kiss – and then moved again to Roseville – and another. At last, I thought, we had a stable, permanent place to live. Then H^2 brought home a camper, a decrepit brown thing that hung over the bed of an old green pickup truck. Jesus, help us.

After a year at California State, the director of EOP advertised for my job again, saying it was required by law. I didn't believe it for a minute. I was the only Anglo on the staff and was ignored repeatedly in conversations and meetings. Discussions among the counselors often involved resentments against America regarding the Japanese internment during World War II and school child abuse in El Paso during the director's childhood. "We weren't allowed to speak Spanish," she complained. Unable to find a replacement for me, I was hired again on a one-year contract. Tired of the insult, I resigned.

After about eight years in California, I knew I had to get back to Texas to try to sort myself out. I wasn't getting along with H^2, who preferred sleeping in the dumpy camper to coming home, and I was drinking on weekends and blaming him for my problems. I had reached the lowest point in my life.

***

Connor, I haven't given many reasons to love my second husband so madly and to stay with him through rum running and mountain peril. His most obvious attraction was his striking good looks. He looked like a movie star. OMG! And he liked me! I couldn't believe it. Heretofore, I had always thought there was something seriously wrong with men who liked me. But he seemed perfect!

And he was brilliant. I was drawn to the way he organized his thoughts when he talked. His conversation was filled with facts—I didn't realize until much later that he made some of them up as he went along. On one occasion, I asked him to identify a ubiquitous kind of tree found in Northern California. His answer began, "There are 26 varieties of eucalyptus trees in California." I thought he had encyclopedic knowledge of just about everything we talked about. He didn't.

H^2 was kind! I hadn't grown up with kind people, neither family nor friends. Children were generally considered a nuisance, and adults were fair game for parody or scorn. He listened with respect to others' ideas; he gave others benefit of the doubt.

Kiss adored him. He was supportive when she dressed as a gypsy for the Halloween costume competition at school, helping her add costume jewelry and a bright scarf for her hair. He wanted to complain to the teacher when she didn't win the prize. I had to hold him back.

There were many good times. At Lake Tahoe's Harrah's Casino, he gave Kiss $100 to play pinball and other arcade games in the supervised children's lounge. He played poker, and I busied myself with blackjack until my brain ran dry. In the winter, the three of us tried skiing. He was great at it; I was pathetic; and Kiss cried if her skis moved on the snow.

We struggled at times to get across the mountains back to Sacramento when the snow came hard and heavy. In our little Toyota coupe, we slipped and slid all over Highway 80. On one such trip back from Tahoe, around Truckee, he tired of dodging other cars and announced to us that he knew a shortcut. Over Donner Pass. In fifth-grade, Kiss had recently studied the wagon train that got stuck in the snow on the way to Oregon and the resulting cannibalism! We went around barricades and road-closed signs onto a small road leading to the Pass. Kiss cried most of the trip because she was scared we were going to have to eat each other.

During all those years, the drinking got worse. H^2 spent less and less time at home, and the subsequent quarrels were painful for all three of us. Demoralized and defeated, I planned to take the dog and Kiss back to Texas. Then my father died, and I left California for good.

Texas Again

My father died on April 13, 1977. I was in Sacramento, planning a run-away to Texas. The news knocked the breath out of me, and I fell to the kitchen floor, unable to stand. H²'s sister rushed to help me. I had planned to leave California on the 15th, taking my daughter and my dog in the old Toyota coupe with all the bumps and bruises from being driven "under the influence." On the 14th, I left California for good and never looked back.

In East Texas once again, I was sure my life was over. My father was gone, my mother was in the black throes of grief, and I had initiated a second divorce. Kiss was twelve and beginning to be a teenage pain in the neck. Never a red-hot coper, I was fully over my head, drowning in fear, failure, and alcoholism.

As spring turned to summer, I spent my time sending applications for learning specialist and reading specialist positions to nearby junior colleges. In the evenings, I drank, draining my father's liquor cabinet. I tried to convince myself I was staying with Mama to help her through this hard time, but the truth was I had nowhere else to go, no job, and few prospects.

I accepted an instructor of English and reading position at Bishop College, a United Negro College Fund college, where most of my students were African American young people from some of America's biggest cities, like Chicago and Detroit. I couldn't hazard a guess about the lives these kids left to study in South Dallas. The faith-based college was supported by the Southern Baptist Church and the United States government.

Almost all the Bishop students received Pell Grants, a program created by the U.S. government in 1972, for support. There was a campus of several buildings. Each Friday a required chapel presented fabulous preachers from all over the country. The structure of their sermons included a thesis, examples, a refrain – repeated throughout – and a conclusion. I taught this composition model to my students and instructed them to take notes outlining the sermon. In class we discussed the presentation and its structure. At lunch I often discussed the message with the preacher himself.

My schedule was bizarre. Three days a week I had a 9:00 class and one later at 4:00. I often left after my morning class and went to downtown Dallas to a bar for drinks. Making my way back to campus, I ate mints and chewed gum in the car to mask my breath. I thought I was successful, but one of my students noticed all was not normal.

"You know what you smell like?" he said.

"No, Larry, what?"

"You smell like a cantaloupe," he said.

Relieved, I realized I had perfumed my breath until I smelled like a fruit salad.

On Tuesdays and Thursdays, my schedule was more compact.

In February, I received an announcement of a fellowship offered by the National Endowment of the Humanities on the "Grammatical Traditions of English." The program would take place at the University of Texas at Austin and award a $2,500 stipend. *Jesus, help me!* I needed this money. Desperate, I figured I was good enough in grammar to apply, so I wrote and rewrote my application essay. After many editions, written over a period of about two weeks, it was ready to submit.

Money difficulties plagued Bishop College. Besides a very low salary, I was forced to buy my own supplies: copy paper, stapler, and paper clips. I was barely treading financial waters. In April of 1978, Bishop College defaulted on instructors' salaries, and we received nothing. The president of the college called a faculty meeting to announce late paychecks, and faculty were to keep the secret. He didn't know when the money would flow again.

Furious, I returned to my office and called the *Dallas Morning News* city desk. Anonymously, I said, "Bishop College did not meet payroll." It hit the front page the next day. The president was livid and vowed to find the whistle blower. I was already furloughed, so I didn't worry about it.

Sobriety

I submitted a check for April's rent. In a panic, I informed the apartment manager of the insufficient funds in my account. When I received no pay again in May, she filed suit against me. The court date was set for early June.

On April 24, 1978, I drank my last drink.

***

The University of Texas English Department called: I was chosen for the fellowship. *Thank you, Jesus.* The first of June, Bishop College paid me for April, and I moved to Austin, where I collected the $2,500. I was safe for the summer, but I had no job for the next school year. A neighbor agreed to go to court in Dallas on my behalf. The judge was not pleased when the apartment manager repeatedly tried to deposit the April rent check. He ordered her to pay all the penalties the bank charged me, and I paid my back rent for April and May.

Austin Again

I arrived in Austin with no prospects of employment for the fall. Financially safe only until September and in a panic, I began to apply for jobs all over the U.S. I even considered applying for a position in an American university in Iran. Other fellows in the workshop discouraged my Iranian plans and began to investigate their own colleges and universities, looking for positions in college reading/learning skills. I was so scared I could hardly think. My worst nightmare was moving in with my mother and/or going on welfare.

The *Austin American Statesman* revealed large quantities of the Pell Grant money embezzled by some administrators of Bishop College. The money, which should have gone to students, created a shortfall of available funds for payroll. The college closed its doors shortly after and ceased operation.

And Connor, I had nothing to do with it!

The first week of seminars, I began my research on Noah Webster and his spelling and grammar books. Spending time in the new Harry Ransome Center, I read Webster's first books, popularly called the *Blue-Back Speller* and something like *A Compendium of English Grammar*. Those little books, published by Webster himself, stayed in print from the time of George Washington to the presidency of Theodore Roosevelt. They went west in covered wagons and provided a text for countless schools as this country expanded to the Pacific Ocean. My question is... what happened to all those books? Thousands, if not millions, of people learned to read and write from them, but there are only a handful left in rare books collections.

Noah Webster was an interesting study. During the time of the American Revolution, he recognized language change, expecting American English to evolve into something different from British English. He wrote the "blue-back speller" and a grammar in his efforts to control those changes.

However, he didn't consider language evolution to be eternal. He tried to prevent the change by formulating rules for spelling and pronunciation. The speller warns Americans against slothful speech habits, such as the ones found in the American South. I'm sure he would have been horrified by my Texas accent. He wrote all kinds of rules for correct American English pronunciation, rules he insisted would not change. His ideal dialect was Southern England.

Around the end of June, I sat in a cage reading Webster's rare books, published in the 1790s, I think. I turned a page and ran across a verse about trusting God: "Consider the lilies of the field, how they grow. They neither toil nor spin, yet Solomon in all his glory was not clothed as one of these." I thought Webster had written it.

In the afternoon I crossed Guadalupe Street to the University Co-op to get my mother a birthday card. There it was again. "Consider the lilies..." At St. David's Episcopal the very next Sunday, the same verse was the lesson of the day: "Think about flowers; they don't have jobs, and God provides for them."

From church I went home and picked up my Bible to read the scripture again. The quotation came from the Gospel of Matthew, the Sermon on the Mount. God takes good care of plants that grow one day and are thrown into an oven the next day. How much more will he care for me?

I pondered this idea. Would it be the end of me if I didn't find a job? I could take Kiss and live with my mother until something turned up. God would provide for all of us. We wouldn't starve or go naked. It wouldn't be how I wanted it to be, but it would work out.

Consider the lilies of the field, how they grow. I got it! His eye is on the sparrow, and I know he watches me.

Instantly I relaxed. Relief flooded me and I made the decision to stop looking for a job. I had applied to several institutions around Texas. I reasoned if God wanted me to have a job, He would find me one I had already applied for. If not, I was willing either to work or to do nothing.

The architects of this democracy called God "Divine Providence." I became willing to trust Providence. I think it was the first time I decided to trust God instead of telling Him what to do. Until then, I had considered God a kind of pinch hitter whose job was to extricate me from whatever bind I had gotten myself into. However, recently God had helped me do the impossible – to stop drinking. I decided to rely on Him and watch what He could do. It took a lot of prayer!

On campus the next day, I ran into one of the fellows from my class. "University of North Carolina has posted a position opening in their learning center," he said.

"North Carolina is too far away," I said. "I'm going to wait for job to open in Texas."

"Last week you were talking about going to Iran!" he said.

"I know it, but I decided to trust God."

"You are so strange."

As it turned out, I received a call from the University of Texas at Arlington [UTA]. They were looking for a learning specialist and I had been recommended by the director of the learning center at UT Austin. I was terrified; so much was riding on this interview. I said something like, "God, come with me and give me the words to say."

Entering the director's office, I saw three counselors and an extra chair, where I imagined God could sit. I answered all questions truthfully. Toward the end of the session, one of the counselors asked, "Why should we hire you, Elizabeth?"

"Because I'm the best qualified," I answered. "But I'll be okay if you don't choose me. I've been down, but I'm on my way up now."

She told me later my answer amazed her. "I've never heard anyone say anything like it in an interview."

I began at UTA in August. I had not missed a paycheck. I was truly on my way up. Unfortunately, Kiss was on her way down.

RJ

After a year in Arlington, I met a man at a neighborhood meeting where he was speaking on something I was probably bored with and so can't remember. After RJ invited me for coffee, it felt natural to continue seeing each other. Because he distracted me from thinking about Husband to the Second Power, I enjoyed spending time with him. His surgery schedule was easy to plan – he didn't take many emergencies – so he had enough time on his hands for movies, restaurants, and other entertainment. He became my new boyfriend.

While my second husband was the love of my life, I admired RJ. I learned he had quit drinking ten years before we met. Perfect. His manners were impeccable, his attitude kind. I marveled at how brave you'd have to be to cut into someone's back to fuse vertebrae together. I loved to talk to him about what he did in the O.R. The best part about his practice was his patients didn't die.

As the UTA Counseling, Testing, and Career Placement learning specialist, I wrote a two-hour non-credit class on power reading college texts. Well received by students, the course concentrated on diluting the text to the salient information in a list format. A student said, "I just hope I can remember all these facts!"

That led me to the question of how to improve students' memories. I didn't recall how I learned to memorize, but I found a couple of books at the university bookstore, *Stop Forgetting* by Bruno Furst and a smaller one, *The Memory Book* by Jerry Lucas. Both showed how to associate one thing with another to remember it.

I began with birthdays and practiced until I got it mostly right. Then I designed a workshop based on making and remembering associations, offering it tentatively to students telling them I wasn't sure it would work. My own memory trick came right out of the book. As students entered the workshop, I marked their first names and their birthdays on a seating chart. Then I used associations to quickly memorize them. I presented the strategies in the books with examples, pros and cons of the method, and finished the workshop with my recitation of each student's name and birthday. They and I were impressed. I hadn't been convinced I could do it.

The next Monday a sophomore chemistry major stopped by my office to report his success. "I tried it before my tennis lesson. The associations took twenty minutes! I planned to return to studying for a big test the next day, but after tennis I was able to recite everything I'd studied. Then I knew I knew it, and I knew I'd know it for as long as I wanted to."

I scheduled several memory workshops throughout the first half of the semester.

An odd thing happened. A man representing Evelyn Wood speed reading gave a sales presentation for UTA students on campus. All I knew about Evelyn Wood was Woody Allen's joke. "I read *War and Peace* in nineteen minutes. It's about Russia," he said.

I decided to go see what they promised. A thin, manic little guy presented himself as a Ph.D. lecturer who could read several books in a day. I listened a while, and, skeptical, I raised my hand and asked where he earned his Ph.D. He gave me the name of a college in West Texas.

"That school doesn't offer graduate degrees," I said.

Mr. Speed Reader exploded. "How dare you come in here and ruin my presentation?" he demanded.

"How dare *you* misrepresent yourself and your ability? These are sincere students trying to improve their study strategies."

I addressed the group of about thirty students and told them to save their money. Oh, and to check out my free workshops offered through the Counseling Office.

Following my memory systems session with one on reading the college text twice as fast, and reading it only once, I received several comments from students who returned to report that their grades had gone up as a direct result of my instruction. The last two-hour class I wrote was writing an essay-test answer. My little noncredit classes filled as soon as I announced them.

At Christmas, I received an invitation to the UTA President's Christmas party and told RJ I didn't want to go, but such a party is usually a command performance. I was like Ensign Pulver in *Mister Roberts*, a hilarious play I had studied in college. Ensign Pulver was a timid Navy man who wanted to stay unnoticed. He hid from the captain, ducking into doors when he saw him coming. However, one day he was climbing the ship's spiral stair when he looked up and saw the captain descending above him.

"Who are you?" the older man asked.

"Ensign Pulver, sir."

"How long have you been on board?"

"Two years, sir."

Like Pulver, I had been hiding. The president and vice president's offices were on the same floor as mine.

RJ laughed and said he would be glad to go with me. The date arrived, and he, wearing a beautiful black suit, white shirt, and red tie, took me to the party. The president and his wife met us at the door and introduced themselves. He gave the president's hand an enthusiastic shake before I could introduce him. As I hung my coat in a closet, I was horrified to see the two men in a huddle, involved in a conversation in a corner of the room. I couldn't hide any more.

When I quit drinking, I learned to *represent* love more than feel it. All my previous relationships were based on self: What's in it for me? Not once had I ever wondered about *my* responsibility in relationships. I hated my sister for marrying

Carl. I wanted to add algebra to the subjects I could deal with, so I married H. After my divorce, I thought I loved H to the Second Power, but he didn't exist in reality – I loved my idea of who I wanted him to be. Resentments ate me alive at my failures to be happy. No, I had never loved anyone, warts and all, as they say.

From our first day, I under-whelmed RJ's mother Anna with my ordinary clothes and plain appearance. A doctor's wife, Anna bought her clothes from a Neiman Marcus personal shopper. The way she looked and talked to me let me know I was not quite up to par.

I was different from Anna in so many ways. I came from a working-class background, had never had any extra money, dressed more like a graduate student than a fashion plate, and so on. I had what she called "unrefined tastes." A recent widow, she was not happy with her lot in life; her husband had died, and her only child had brought home an alien.

Accepting the challenge, I resolved to be the best friend to her I could be. I had quit drinking alcohol and smoking funny cigarettes when I was thirty-eight; I had joined the staff of a big department at a major university. Therefore, I felt bulletproof at forty. A little old lady would never get the best of me. I had changed.

I think RJ's problem with Anna's drinking lay in her lack of hearing. She never had more than a glass of wine, but she drove him crazy. Placing her flat hand beside her mouth to unsuccessfully mute the sound, she announced her loud criticism of the people around us. The single glass of wine often precipitated an under-the-table pitched battle of pokes and small slaps between them. Because they couldn't leave each other alone, I learned to sit between them and referee their squabbles.

Kiss

In the year and a half since I'd quit drinking alcohol, my life began to work out professionally. However, my personal life was circling the toilet bowl. Kiss continued to get more out of control. She stopped attending school, began experimenting with drugs, and regularly left home and Arlington without official leave. I could feel myself coming apart, crying, anxious, restless.

The sheriff's department of another town notified me that Kiss was in jail. When I got there, she wouldn't talk to me. She refused to come with me. The police delivered her to a treatment center in Arlington, but she refused recovery. When she got out of the hospital, it was more of the same. I felt like I was made of glass, and any strong bump would shatter me.

RJ was sympathetic. He asked me to marry him. "Let me take care of you while you take care of her," he said.

Once again, I married a man I wasn't in love with. What was wrong with me? I married Husband to the Third Power. In May I took a year's leave of absence from UTA.

Anna was 80; Third Power was 60; I was forty. Anna, probably anticipating the marriage to fail, didn't have a lot of time to waste getting to know and like me. At every turn she did not try to hide her criticism.

Moving to Fort Worth, I joined Third Power first in his apartment and then into a 1915 home we bought in the hospital district. We lived there a few months and then moved to the west side of Ft. Worth to a split-level ranch style on top of a hill overlooking the Air Force base.

Anna lived across town on the south side. "You never wear a dress," she observed correctly. I didn't bother to defend my choice of clothes because everyone knows a teacher's budget won't accommodate NM dresses. "You should wear your hair like Princess Di." I couldn't see it. My hair was more like Queen Elizabeth's, and I didn't care. However, her barrage of suggestions led me to consider some of her ideas.

After Third Power and I married, I allowed Anna to take me to Neiman's in Fort Worth and let her personal shopper bring scores of dresses to the changing room. As we stepped off the escalator and turned toward the *haute couture* corner of the second floor, I learned what the walking farts are. Every time Anna's right foot hit the carpet, she rumbled too loud not to hear. However, she couldn't hear it thunder, so, nonplussed, she walked unapologetically ahead of me.

Among an embarrassment of beautiful dresses, the two fashionistas chose a blue dress with tiny flowers. They agreed the fit was right, the color perfect. When I met Third Power later, I told him I would not be returning to Neiman's because his mother had embarrassed me.

"She's humiliated me for 60 years," he said. "You'll get used to it."

Being married to the two of them was fun at first. I was never at a loss for stories to tell Connie and Sally. Third Power, his mother, and I often went to big parties held by local, state, and national medical associations. I always wore my blue dress to please Anna. Third Power and I didn't drink alcohol, but Anna liked a glass of wine with her dinner.

At a festive occasion at the Colonial Country Club, Anna put her hand to her mouth and said of the couple across from us, "I think that's his fourth wife." I thought it was hilarious; after all, she wasn't *my* mother. The proclamation about the other doctor and his fourth wife visibly upset Third Power, who announced it was time to go before dessert. He disappeared to fetch the car, leaving Anna and me to negotiate the colossal staircase down into the elegant lobby of the Colonial. Recalling her glass of wine, I took her hand halfway down. With the other hand, she placed her flat palm across her mouth and exclaimed, "Look at the stomach on that man!" Every man in the huge lobby looked down at his belly.

Anna had two sisters, Ella, who was almost completely deaf, and Wanda, who repeated in a shout for Ella everything anybody said. An element of riotous fun was added when all three were together. I planned at least one weekly activity with them. Third Power would meet us for lunch, and I would collect the sisters.

One day, arriving at the new Peony Chinese restaurant, we discovered a large square room with occupied tables all around the four walls. A waiter seated us in the center of the huge room. The look on Third Power's face revealed a fear of being on display; it would not turn out well.

Taking our seats, Wanda said, "If you want good Chinese food, you need to go to Jimmie Dip's."

"Wha'd she say?" Ella said.

"Jimmie Dip's," Wanda repeated, a little louder.

"What?" Ella said.

"I said if you want good Chinese food, you need to go to Jimmie Dip's!" Wanda shouted.

All eyes were now on us. Glancing at Third Power, I discovered him with *The Journal of the American Medical Association* covering his face.

On the way back to her house, Anna opened her purse and held in her hand a small, lipstick-size object. I was driving, so I couldn't see in the back seat. "What is it?" I asked.

"It's mace," she said, "to protect me when I'm out."

"What?" Ella said.

"It's mace to protect her," Wanda yelled.

Afraid she was going to set off her mace device causing us to crash the car and die, I kept repeating for her to put it back into her purse.

"To activate it, you just have to push this button," Anna said.

"Activate the button," Wanda said. They passed it back and forth among themselves, looking at it.

So it went all the way back to Anna's house. I couldn't see what they were doing with the mace. Anna didn't get it back into her purse until Wanda and Ella had both held and examined it. When we finally turned into her driveway, I was a wreck.

Later, I told Third Power about the incident. Suspicion clouding his face, he said, "I think you enjoy this."

"I live for it," I assured him.

During the holidays, he offered to take the sisters on a tour of holiday lights in downtown Fort Worth, ending with dinner at the Fort Worth Club. Third Power suggested we take the motor home because of its big windows and 360-degree view. Anna, Ella, and Wanda were waiting for us, dressed in their finest, sparkling with jewelry. Third Power wore a beautiful suit, and I wore a Christmas-y red dress.

When we arrived, Anna visually assessed my appearance, frowning.

"You're late," she said.

"Ten minutes," I said

"Do you ever wear the blue dress you bought at Neiman's?"

"I wear it so often I'm afraid people will think it's the only one I have." She didn't look pleased.

I have never heard so much complaining as on this festive occasion. Each year, Fort Worth goes all out for the holidays. From Thanksgiving to the end of the Stock Show in January, white lights outline the downtown skyscrapers in the dark.

Anna said, "The motor home is too high to step up to get in."

"What?" Ella said.

Wanda said, *"She said it's too hard to get in."*

From getting into the motor home to getting out at the Fort Worth Club, the grousing never stopped.

"Don't drive so fast."

"Don't drive so fast."

"This seat is uncomfortable."

"This seat is uncomfortable."

For the first time, I took pity on Third Power. Helping Anna step down, I said, "You ought to be ashamed of yourself. He has busted his butt to give you and your sisters a festive night out, and the three of you have done nothing but complain." To her credit, the complaints stopped.

Shortly after we wed, I quit smoking. I was embarrassed to be married to a medical doctor and smoke cigarettes. I had tried for years to ditch the habit. I quit for two years before H and I divorced, then started back. I lasted six months several times. A friend had told me one drink is too many and a thousand aren't enough. I learned it was true of cigarettes, too.

Jesus and I began a final campaign against my nicotine addiction. Tobacco proved a harder habit to break than alcohol. My body screamed for nicotine, day after day. My skin crawled; I had headaches; my fingernails and hair hurt. Through it all, I repeated my mantra, "One day at a time. I won't smoke today, but I might smoke tomorrow." Fortunately, on the days after, I didn't want to smoke. There were times I sat on my hands to stop shaking. I cried, hating myself for being a slave to cigarettes. News came out that cigarette manufacturers were adding chemicals to the tobacco to make them more addictive, triggering a huge surge of stubborn resolve in my attitude. I would not give in to those greedy bastards.

I bought a needlepoint kit at Michael's. Reading the directions and studying the illustrations helped me master one stitch, the basket weave. Sewing several hours a day kept my hands busy. I prayed for strength. Sometimes I had to endure a few minutes at a time. When I craved nicotine, I promised God I wouldn't smoke until I finished the row I was working on. Then I forgot and started a new row. Finishing one project, I'd begin the next one immediately. After two weeks, I felt like I had turned a corner on the addiction.

We'd been married about a year when Anna was robbed. Ironically, another doctor's daughter broke into her house and took her jewelry and sterling silver. She called me as soon as she arrived home and discovered the broken window. I told her to call the police. By the time I could rush to her, the cops were there, fingerprinting and photographing damage. Several officers walked around the apartment smoking cigarettes. Head down, face in hands, looking small and defeated, Anna was distraught in her yellow wingback chair with a bedsheet covering the cushion. She could hardly answer the questions posed by the officer in charge. I wanted, no, I *needed* a cigarette! *Jesus, help me.*

I called Third Power, who arrived a few minutes later. When police left and we were sure Anna would be all right, he returned to his office full of patients, and I went home. In the car, I remembered a partial pack of Marlboros in a kitchen drawer, left by a friend a few weeks earlier. I hurried into the kitchen and flung the drawer open. Cigarettes in hand, I was about to take one out of the pack when I heard a voice inside my head say, *"Do you really want to quit?"*

I stopped. *Yes*, I thought, *I really do.*

After running water on the cigarettes, I left the kitchen for the bedroom where I changed into my nightgown. It was 3:00 P.M. I couldn't pursue an impulse to the convenience store to buy cigarettes without changing clothes. Then I started to work on a needlepoint project to keep my hands busy, praying for help with an overpowering desire for nicotine. Jesus and I made it through my unhappy day using a one-day-at-a-time strategy: *If God wants me to die from wanting a cigarette, this is a good day for it. I won't smoke today, but if I feel like this tomorrow, I might.* The next day the craving was gone forever.

About three months later, Anna's doctor diagnosed breast cancer. Inoperable. I drove her to devastating infusions of chemotherapy which caused horrific sores in her mouth. Arriving at the cancer treatment facility, she did not sit in the waiting room. Instead, she stood at the reception desk and waited, one hand on her hip, demonstrating an expectation of immediate service. They took her right in to the treatment room.

Anna began to lose weight, and I baked bread and rolls to tempt her to eat. I bought her a cantaloupe from Peru at Roy Pope's, Fort Worth's precursor to Whole Foods. After chemo, she suffered through radiation therapy daily for six weeks. One day when I called to tell her I was on my way, she said, "Don't bring any more food. I'm giving it away to the neighbors."

To cheer his mother, Third Power traded her Chevrolet for a yellow Cadillac Seville. She loved it, and when the radiation treatments ended, she again joined her friends at the bridge table and lunch circuit. She felt much better, and we all resumed our outings with the sisters. Life was good for about eighteen more months.

Then Anna's cancer returned with a vengeance, necessitating several emergency trips to the doctor's office and the hospital for pain control. Ahead of our arrival time, I called the ER and asked them to come with a wheelchair to take her inside. Then, after parking the car in the doctors' parking lot, I went inside to help her. Clutching the arms of the wheelchair, she said, "This is it!"

"This is not it," I said. "We're just here to help you with your pain."

Pushing her to her assigned room, I did what I could to get her settled in. The nursing staff knew her: she was Third Power's mother and worthy of royal treatment. Once in her hospital bed, Anna had instructions for me. "Pull the blanket up over my feet." Then, "Not so high." Then, "Up a little bit."

The next day, a nurse called me to say Anna was ready to be discharged. In shorts and tee shirt, I dropped everything and ran to collect her. The nurse had wheeled her to the entrance and waited with her.

After about a minute in the car, she said, "You look like a two-year-old."

"Well, Anna, you have a choice to make," I said. "You can either let me take you home, or I can take you back to the ER where you can find someone better dressed." Enough said.

The hospital stays grew longer and more frequent as time went on, and Anna's suffering became more obvious. Her lungs filled with liquid, making it difficult to breathe. She could scarcely get comfortable. Her doctor, a Lebanese surgeon – she asked me if I thought he was lesbian – drained some of the liquid through a tube inserted into her side.

Each day when I visited her room, she appeared smaller and weaker. I prayed to God to accompany me as I opened her door. One day I found her unmoving. Terrified she was dead, I did the "look, listen, and feel" tactic I learned in CPR classes, I bent low over her chest to detect chest movement. Nothing. I put my face close to her chest but couldn't see her breathe. Finally, I moved in closer to see if I could feel her breath on my face.

When our noses were less than an inch apart, she opened her eyes.

"Who did your hair?" she asked.

"I did," I said.

"I like it," was her first positive comment on my appearance.

Eventually we had to look for a nursing facility for her. Third Power signed her into one not far from the hospital, and I drove too fast because she could receive no oxygen in my car. The place was crowded; she had a roommate; and the tiny room smelled of urine. It was horrible.

"Anna," I said. "Stay here with the oxygen. I'm going to find you a better place."

I had some trouble convincing Third Power I could not leave his mother there. "If you don't help me find a good nursing home for her," I said, "I will bring her home with me and take care of her myself." That did it. He made a few calls and found a clean facility with a large private room with a patio.

"I can die here," she said, settling in.

"Can you live here?" I asked.

She didn't answer.

Anna lived almost a week longer. Each day I went to her room with my needlepoint. I helped her every way possible: ice water, tissues, and other incidentals. She hardly ate anything at all. I sat in a reasonably comfortable chair, working the needlepoint basketweave stitch diagonally across a large canvas.

There was a prayer I learned from Agnes Sanford, a true believer in the healing power of prayer. In her autobiography, *Sealed Orders*, she prescribed a repetition prayer: "Jesus Christ, Son of God, Savior, have mercy on me." I prayed this prayer-without-ceasing, substituting "Anna" for myself. On Saturday, the day before she died, she moaned, and I asked her if she needed something for pain.

"No," she said. "I don't have any pain." God is merciful.

We received the call at 3:00 A.M. on Sunday. On Monday, I learned the funeral home was booked for the next week, but we could get a timeslot for Tuesday. Wanda and Ella complained loudly about the rush to bury their sister. I wasn't happy about it either.

In the weeks after the funeral, while Third Power performed his surgeries downtown, I sorted through her things, making sure sisters and somewhat estranged children received what they wanted. My daughter and I took the few pieces of furniture they left in her apartment. Those pieces occupy honored places in our homes today; I sleep in Anna's bed every night.

In her desk I found pieces of text she had clipped from various books and newsletters, recipes, and prayers asking God for peace, praising God for the beauty of the earth, and thanking God for all her blessings.

At a medical auxiliary meeting, I overheard some of Anna's friends discussing her daughter-in-law, *me*, in glowing terms. They said I had gone further for her than anyone could have predicted; I had done for her what they hoped their adult children would do for them; and I had encouraged her to carry on.

I had loved her, warts and all.

What Came Next?

After my leave of absence from UTA, I didn't return to teaching full time for several years. Instead, I joined the adjunct faculty of a local community college teaching English composition. I wrote several non-credit continuing education courses for UTA: studying for the verbal sections of the SAT and graduate school entrance tests, like the GRE and the GMAT.

In the late 1980s, I was writing proposals and instructional materials for the Justice Department on behalf of the Association for Retarded Citizens National Headquarters in Arlington. I wrote a couple of pamphlets on fetal alcohol syndrome, but my main contribution was a set of materials including a book, a video, a board game, and lesson plans on the U.S. Constitution designed for high school students with mild retardation and funded by the U.S. Department of Justice. I loved working part time; I could have days off if I wanted to, and time for travel between writing jobs.

During this time, Kiss remained as wild as a March hare. I seldom knew where she was and never *how* she was. We were incommunicado. Then I got a message that she was getting married and requested my presence at the wedding. At first, I thought of not going, but my friend Eloise insisted that she would go with me. That was the beginning, however shaky, of our reconciliation.

The short form of the story over the next few years is Kiss got married, had a baby, divorced, married again, and had two more babies. My first grandchild was Shannon. The pregnancy was dangerous and scary. Kiss' placenta calcified, and we were at the doctor's office every day at the end for a sonogram. Finally, on the 27th of June 1983, the doctor announced that we would have a Caesarian birth the next day.

"The placenta will no longer sustain life. There is a chance that this little boy will be growth retarded and possibly mentally retarded." We left crying.

That night, we knelt in prayer. "Father, we know you know how to make babies, and we are asking for one of your very best in Jesus' name. Amen." We cried ourselves to sleep.

The next morning at the hospital, I checked Kiss in and went to the gift shop and bought a blue teddy bear. After a wait of about two hours, a nurse came out and announced, "You have a baby girl."

Thinking she was talking to one of the other visitors in the waiting room, I sat back down.

"No," she said, looking at me. "*You* have a baby girl." Several months of planning for a boy baby, including two weeks of daily sonograms, and we were all wrong about the sex of the child. How could that be? I prefer to think that my Heavenly Father replaced that little boy with one of His best: Shannon, a near-perfect baby, with an Apgar score of nine.

The Open Road

It took a long time for Third Power to sell me on a recreational vehicle. He won me over when he pointed out that we could keep our stuff in one place and not pack and unpack for each new destination. We shopped locally for our perfect travel home.

The salesman said, "This is a lovely RV; it sleeps six." The floor space was less than my closet at home.

"And it sleeps six!" he repeated. "Just turn the couch into bunk beds and pull this table down and put a mattress on it."

I didn't know six people I liked well enough to crowd into this tiny space. I doubted whether I liked Third Power that much. We kept looking. Keen to travel, he reminded me of how great it would be to visit other states and meet new friends from all over the U.S. I should have been suspicious: he didn't much like other people. We finally found a winner, a slightly used 1979 GMC motor home with 25,000 miles on it.

Our first trip was to Santa Fe, New Mexico, where the closest campground was about ten miles east of town. There were two problems with Santa Fe. First, to go into the city from the campground, we had to unhook the water and electricity and drive the bus-size behemoth on crowded, narrow streets. A nightmare. Second, the people around the campfire the first night were mostly from Fort Worth.

"I could have met them at Safeway," I said. We had to go back to the planning stage for a successful travel experience.

Next up was an international doctors' conference in British Columbia, Canada. Third Power bought a 1965 VW Beetle to pull behind the motorhome to make us more mobile. We loved the little car, but it often broke down, and repairs cost a fortune.

The next trip we took was to San Diego. Somewhere in Arizona the Beetle died, and we donated it on the spot to Goodwill. When we returned to Fort Worth, Third Power bought a new compact car to pull behind us on our trips. We often joined a group of friends on weekend excursions to Texas state parks. Those times were wonderful.

When he was away from the office and surgery, Third Power was relaxed and fun, much more energetic than I was. We chartered a boat in Florida and entered a fishing contest. He caught the winning fish although his victory was overshadowed by the storm that kept everyone else out of the contest. We also had a charter on Lake Mead in Nevada, where I caught all the fish. That can be explained by the fact that the professional fisherman and owner of the boat baited my hook, cast out, and handed me the pole when a fish was on the line. We drove our little home to New Orleans and the World's Fair. One of those days we wore pedometers that measured eleven miles walked in the park.

Life was good.

The End of Something Good

Sometime around the middle 1980s, tragedy struck during an ice storm in Fort Worth. Early one morning I heard our doorbell ringing again and again. I roused myself out of bed, noticing I was alone in the bedroom. Opening the front door leading to the stairs down to the garage, I saw our neighbor and his teenage son trying to hold my husband upright and help him up the steps. His face was swollen and bloody, and his right eye was already shut. He was dazed and didn't know where he was.

"Call an ambulance," the man said.

In about fifteen minutes, a siren squealed to our driveway, but it was a fire engine. The paramedics said the ambulance slid off into a ditch when it left its garage. I don't recall everything the paramedics said, but I do remember they couldn't take Third Power to a hospital because they lacked proper transportation. They told me to call a doctor and get instructions.

The neighbor said his son happened to be looking out the front window at the ice when he said, "Oh, Dr. Howard is going out to pick up the paper in his shortie pajamas." Then he said, "Oh, Dr. Howard slipped down on the icy driveway.

"Dad, Dr. Howard is not getting back up." The two of them crossed the street and helped Third Power get into the house. Third Power slept. And slept.

I called a close friend, Dr. G., a neurologist. "Don't let him go to sleep," he said.

After two days, I told Dr. G, "You come over here and keep Rip van Winkle awake. I can't do it."

"Keep trying," he said.

In the meantime, another friend called and said she had no power, water, or heat. I told her to come stay with us and help me figure out what to do about Third Power. She and I spent afternoons sitting on the floor in front of the fire playing Scrabble and trying to wake my husband. When we touched him and talked to him, he opened his eyes and uttered the worst language I ever heard. I got scared because this was new behavior; he seldom cursed.

Dr. G. said, "Not good."

After the head injury, Third Power was a different person. He became paranoid, sure I was out to do him in. "I'm your best friend," I assured him. Truth is, after he insulted and bullied everybody else, I was his *only* friend. Still, he accused me of lying to him, meeting with other men, being a lesbian, and many other "crimes" I can't remember. He abruptly closed his practice, calling another orthopedist to take over his patients still in the hospital. While most doctors retire, he just shut down about six weeks after the accident.

And he began to eat! At night he would get out of bed and go to the kitchen. It became usual for him to consume a loaf of bread and a jar of mayonnaise overnight. In the day, he insisted I serve low-calorie meals, but I would wake in the morning to a kitchen cabinet covered with honey, mayo, and breadcrumbs. His weight ballooned, and the fatter he got, the meaner.

When his office manager and I were left to sort out the office, we discovered he had cashed several big insurance checks without indicating which patients' surgeries they reimbursed. We had no way of knowing whose bills had been paid. There were $300,000 in unpaid bills we had to write off. When we closed the office for the last time, I told the office manager to tell the truth to whoever asked about the office cash flow. "We won't go to jail for this mess," I said.

Life at the Lake

The next couple of years saw a disintegration of everything good the marriage had been. There were no more sweet moments. Third Power was furious at me most of the time because of imagined attitudes against him. He insisted we sell our home and move to the lake to save money. At Lake Whitney, of course, things were no better.

My friend Barbara recommended a local, Jeff, to be our handyman. He charged $4 per hour, and she assured me he was honest. Ordinarily, Jeff wasn't a man you'd hire. He seldom bathed and never washed his clothes. He lived in a ramshackle hut with his dogs, several German shepherds.

Jeff talked a lot. Too much, really. The first day, he kept up a chatter I only half listened to. When he mentioned Lee Harvey Oswald and Jack Ruby in the same sentence, I stopped in my tracks and said, "What are you talking about?"

He explained he was a transvestite, although he didn't use the word. He had often frequented Jack Ruby's nightclub where other transvestites partied. He liked to dress in women's clothes, he said, and would appreciate it if I could partially pay him in pantyhose.

"I don't know, Jeff," I said. "I need to discuss this with my husband." I expected trouble.

Third Power, however, was delighted. As an orthopedic surgeon, he could get super deals on pantyhose. "Absolutely," he said. It was decided: I would supply Jeff with hosiery and occasionally shop for him for shorts and blouses, size 12.

Although there was a problem with Jeff's body odor, he was a sweet man, and I kept him on my payroll. One of the most touching things he did was to nurse a discarded, dead chrysanthemum from a tiny green spark of life in a big brown bush to a thriving show of purple color on the back porch. Jesus said, "By their fruits you will know them." Jeff revealed his character by his tenderness with his dogs and his care of all living things.

I soon adopted a puppy dumped on a country road near us. Third Power named her Mickey. Jeff, a dog lover himself, helped me raise her. He allowed the puppy to "help" him when he did the flower beds. He planted something, and Mickey Howard pulled it out of the ground and laid it beside the hole. Jeff brought the dog to me and asked if she could stay inside awhile. When she got bored and rowdy, I put her out and let Jeff deal with her again.

Connor, your mother, Shannon, was about five or six. On one of her visits, she and I took Mickey to the vet to be spayed. Shannon asked why she had to be spayed, and I said I couldn't cope with puppies.

"I can cope with puppies!" she said.

As she grew, Mickey became more and more unusual. I thought she was a mix between a yellow lab and a German shepherd, but it turned out she was a Rhodesian ridgeback mix, a breed used to fight lions in Africa. Very territorial, she didn't want anyone to get close to me. She chased animals away, howling at squirrels and raccoons as she ran after them. She was not scared of anything; twice she charged huge dogs. Years later, when Kiss' dog Jaime had puppies, Mickey challenged the new mother to a duel more than once. Jaime, a registered black lab twice Mickey's size, beat her up badly. Jaime's mate, Bo, was in love with Mickey, but when he sniffed around her tail, she would attack him.

At the lake, Mickey loved to hate cats and kept them off our property. People abandoned cats out in the country, millions of them. They found our swimming pool to drink out of. Always on duty, Mickey put a stop to that.

And she adored me.

Third Power began to drive to Dallas and back every day to work for the Social Security Administration where he evaluated claims for disability. I was glad he was out of the house all day. The money was irrelevant; I was paying all the bills from my salary writing for the ARC.

His commute was long, almost two hours each way. By the time he got home, he was furious with me. One day he said, "I think you like Mickey more than you like me." I thought it over and discovered I had grown not to like him much at all. On a particularly harrowing day, he returned home complaining about Mickey pulling bark off our trees. "I think I'll have her put down," he said.

"Why don't you do that?" I said. "Let's see what it does for our marriage." Then he left her alone.

A short time after we moved to the lake, he decided we needed a separate garage for our boat, a small pontoon number perfect for toodling around the lake. He liked to fish, but I don't remember him ever catching anything. I read a book while he fiddled with line and tackle.

To satisfy his need for another garage, Third Power ordered a do-it-yourself kit. Days later, an eighteen-wheeler pulled onto our patch of bluebonnets and deposited a huge load of lumber, windows, shingles, and nails, along with instructions for putting it all together. Then he left for Dallas.

"What am I supposed to do with this?" I said.

"Get Jeff to help you," Third Power said.

Connor, why did I try to rise to that occasion? I'm not even good at puzzles. Neither Jeff nor I could have built a wooden box, much less a garage, but to his credit, Jeff followed the directions and laid the foundation and framed the structure. Each stake he put down for the foundation, Mickey dutifully pulled up and laid beside the hole. It took about three months to complete, and when Jeff was done, it looked like a garage, but it wasn't stable. I was afraid the first real wind would take it to Louisiana.

Jeff found a drunk out-of-work carpenter in Whitney who agreed to look at it. The man was from Cuba and spoke very little English. I heard him talking loud and fast to Jeff in either Spanish or English sounding like Spanish. Every once in a while, I recognized a word like *frame* or *plumb*. He spent several days hammering before he announced the project completed.

The boat was too tall to fit through the door of the new garage.

One day in December 1988, Third Power dropped me off in Fort Worth to pick up my car at the dealership service. As I drove away, I realized I had an evening class on SAT preparation beginning in a couple of weeks at UTA's Continuing Education Department. I drove to Arlington to the University bookstore to order texts for the session. This made me get home later by about two hours.

When I entered the house, the phone was ringing. I rushed to answer it to find Third Power demanding to know where I had been. I said I went to the UTA bookstore.

"You said you were going straight home and you didn't! WHERE WERE YOU?"

"I told you where I was," I said. "I wasn't doing anything wrong."

On Saturday, as I was preparing dinner, there was a phone call for Third Power. I looked outside and saw his car, but when I called his name, he didn't answer. I went to the back yard and looked. Not there. Not in the garage, either. I told the caller I would give him a message to return the call and hung up the phone. It was getting dark when I called my friend Barbara to come help me look for him. I worried I would find him in the woods. As I turned away from the phone, I saw his foot. He was sitting just outside the back door.

Opening the door, I said, "Why didn't you answer when I called?"

"Why didn't I answer?" he said in a mocking voice.

"I was worried," I said. "I didn't know where you were."

"Now you know how it feels," he said.

"Are you retaliating against me for going to the University Wednesday?"

By this time, we were both attending his sessions with his psychiatrist. When I reported his mean-spirited behavior each week, the shrink asked him, "What were you thinking?"

It was obvious Third Power was filled with anger toward me. I tried to convince him I was on his side, that I was his best friend. However, nothing convinced him I was not out to destroy him. I started to see a psychologist to alleviate my fear. Along the way, I resolved to take no more abuse. I was done.

I had a meeting in San Antonio coming up with the textbook company I occasionally represented. The Dallas manager reserved a group of rooms for the dozen or so of us present. At the time I was researching the Texas-mandated English curriculum for the company, so after dinner the first night, I returned to my room to work, leaving most of the others conversing in the hotel bar. My phone rang.

The craziness escalated. My very sick husband called a representative of the textbook company and said I was having an affair with the boss. He had been calling the hotel, but all registrations were in a block in the manager's name. I apologized to my friend and said my husband had "lost it."

"I'll call him right away." I did call, but he didn't answer. I could imagine him sitting by the phone crying, afraid to pick up because I might be angry at him. I called a mutual friend to go check on him to be sure he was all right.

At the next appointment, the shrink asked Third Power, "What were you thinking?"

Doctor of Philosophy

On January 1, 1989, Barbara and I walked our usual three miles, discussing a mental-health principle: "If you find yourself in an unhappy situation and don't know what to do, stay there until either the situation changes, or you change." In other words, don't do anything.

Desperate to avoid a third divorce, I pledged to Barbara to stay where I was, one day at a time, until something changed. I really expected me to change and adapt to the craziness. However, about three days later, Third Power woke me during the night beating a tennis racket on the bed in the guest bedroom, yelling, "I'm angry!" several times. I could almost feel the blows.

In a flash I understood my life was no longer about me, but him, what his mood was, what he was doing or not doing, his anger, compulsive eating, retaliating against me for perceived slights. I could feel my time and my strength disappear, and I became unwilling to roll over and play dead. The next day I called an attorney and filed for divorce. I knew it was the right thing to do. Then I ran away from home.

I re-entered U.T. for a Ph.D. Required to pass the Graduate Record Exam, I knew I needed help with the math half of the test; therefore, I studied a GRE video preparation disc in a panic. One question type was to compute the length of one of the sides of a triangle. I think they called it the hypotenuse. I couldn't figure it out, but after studying it awhile, I learned to guess the right answer based on the appearance of the triangle.

I took the test in Round Rock. Inside the auditorium, tanked up on coffee, the first thing I had to do was ask the proctor to let me sit somewhere else, away from the student who was sniffing every second. I could just see myself stabbing him in the eye with my extra No. 2 pencil.

Sitting in a new assigned desk, I said a prayer: "Jesus, I know you know mathematics. I need 1100 points on this exam." Jesus and I made 1120. The University of Texas at Austin Graduate School admitted me.

I had no idea how I would live in Austin, but barriers fell, one by one. The College of Education awarded me a job as student teacher supervisor. I found a small three-bedroom house with a fenced backyard for Mickey Howard and me. Jeff helped me move my belongings, making sure I understood he was working for me, not Third Power, whom he had grown to dislike. I settled in.

In my first class, beginning statistics, I got to the classroom early and staked out my seat on the front row, almost nauseated from fear and dread of mathematics. You could take two of your courses pass-fail, which I saw as a possible way to advance to the next semester. The professor blew in like the west wind and drew a huge Greek sigma on the board first thing. Having no clue what a sigma meant, I teared up, thinking, *I am so screwed*.

After about a week, however, I realized statistics dealt with probability and correlation with little or no use of long division or the multiplication tables. The reasoning behind each problem made a modicum of sense. Of course, this was before students were allowed to use calculators, so the class wasn't exactly easy for me. I studied hard and earned a "pass." I got through the research statistics course the same way: "pass." The rest of my grades were good.

I continued to write curriculum for ARC National Headquarters and to represent a national textbook company for the adoption of English literature books for Texas public schools. I wrote a brochure for a retired police organization and one for the UT Methodist student center. Taking summers off, I rested my 50-year-old self.

After three years of classes, my dissertation took two years to research and write. I interviewed ten high school teachers in Round Rock Independent School District, seeking their attitudes and practices in the wake of the newest requirements of standardized curriculum and tests. I discovered teachers sometimes ignored the required standards and hated the tests. They mostly continued to teach concepts they considered most important and considered the amount of time students practiced for the tests a waste.

In my research, I discovered one further principle: The tests and the standards covered different curricula. Concepts covered on the tests might not appear in the required curriculum, and conversely, the required curriculum might not be assessed in the tests.

After four and a half years, I graduated with a Ph.D. in curriculum and instruction, completing all the English and reading education courses, in addition to required subjects and writing a dissertation entitled *Teachers' Planning Styles in the Context of Mandated Curriculum.*

Kiss and Ben hosted a dinner party for me the day of graduation in May 1993. Wearing a black robe, an orange velvet cape, and a perky black velvet hat, I attended the outdoor Graduate School ceremony, too excited to realize how hot I was. I also didn't know I was emotionally burned out. They call the Ph.D. the terminal degree, I think because, like a terminal disease, it's the end.

Austin Science Academy

The day after I graduated, I began a job search. Because of my Texas accent, I imagined I would fit best in a Southern university, but northerners liked me more. I went to interview in Flint, Michigan, and Toledo, Ohio, but I realized I don't know how to live where it's cold. There was talk of lake-effect snow and harrowing commutes. Then I had a phone interview with a community college in Massachusetts. Later I received a call from the director of the Science Academy of Austin.

"Your name was given to me by Dr. Farrell," she said. "He said you are a good writer, and we need someone to write our curriculum."

"I don't know anything about science," I said. "I don't think I'm your person."

"It's okay," she said, "we know the science; we just want you to write the curriculum as the teachers describe it to you."

I loved working with the Science Academy students. Different from the ones I was accustomed to, these kids were at the top of the achievement scale. Several made perfect scores on the SAT each year. They built and repaired the school's computers. The math club won first in most Texas math tournaments and in many national ones. The calculus teacher usually had top scores for his AP calculus classes; sometimes everyone in the class earned a perfect 5.

One day the FBI arrived at my office looking for a student. I checked the schedule and walked down to the class to get him. I was more nervous than he was. "The FBI!" I said. "What did you do?"

"I hacked into Norton," he said. Norton was one of the top electronic security companies. They protected people against hacking.

"Why?" I said.

"Just to see if I could," he replied.

I never found out what happened to our hacker.

During the summer, after a year at the Austin Science Academy, I accepted a position as assistant professor of secondary education at Arizona State University West in Phoenix. The chairman of my dissertation committee agreed it was the right thing to do. "You don't need a Ph.D. to be curriculum coordinator at the Science Academy," he said.

For job satisfaction, I should have stayed in Austin.

Mary Dorothy Mitchell

Connor, ours was a close family despite the 250 miles between Galveston and East Texas. We often went for weekends and holidays for visits with aunts, uncles, cousins, and old family friends. I was right in the middle of the cousins' birth order, four older and four younger. My mother had two brothers, David and Dan, and two sisters. The brothers had two children each. David and Mary's children were Mary Dorothy, two years my junior, and David Thomas, born two years later. Mary Dorothy had Down Syndrome.

Dan and Dorothy's children were Martha and John, four and six years younger than I. Caroline and Joe lost their second born, a son named Jefferson McCasland, to measles and whooping cough. Jo Carol, their older child, lived, and lives still as I write this. She's 90, I think. Jo Carol and Frances were born eight days apart. Mary Lou, the youngest of my mother's four, was the mother of Wilma Jean, who was three when I was born.

I've always felt cheated out of two cousins because of Down Syndrome and measles. The rest of us are well educated, intelligent, and interesting people. I wonder what the two of them would be like had they been allowed to live.

When I was four and Mary Dorothy was two, Mama said I was responsible for her when we played together. I was conscious of her limited cognitive ability, and I watched her closely. Once in Jefferson, when we were five and three, she disappeared briefly from my sight. I found her in a bedroom holding an open bottle of my uncle's heart medication. Taking her by the hand, I led her to the room where the adults were talking and told them what I'd found. Panic ensued. The result was a stomach pump at the hospital for my tiny cousin. She had ingested several of the tablets.

Elizabeth Howard

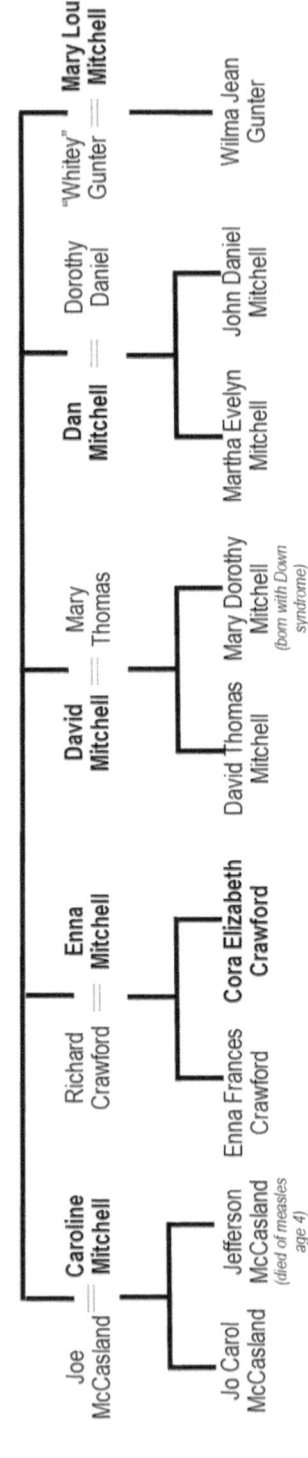

There was no special education, no school for Mary Dorothy to attend. Through the years, Aunt Mary homeschooled her, teaching her to read and to behave herself. She was headstrong. And just plain strong. As a child, I couldn't take her hand and make her go where I wanted her to. I had to sell her on the idea of going to the next room or outside, or wherever. If I hurried to her and grabbed her hand to take her to another place, she was as stationary as a statue. I couldn't move her.

As we grew, she developed a love of actors. These were days before television, so I assume her mother took her to the movies. She carried Hollywood magazines around and could recite details about her favorite heroes, always men. She loved men. After the advent of television, which considerably broadened her horizons, she loved the man who played the lead on "Hawaii Five-Oh." Carrying a magazine in her hand throughout the day, she read articles about actors and had an astonishing memory for facts in the lives of the Hollywood elite.

Aunt Mary died of breast cancer in 1961; Mary Dorothy was nineteen. I had just started to teach, and my life began to consume me. There was little contact with her for several years. Eventually, she moved into a state facility when Uncle David could no longer care for her. The family thought it was best for her. Today I disagree.

Fast forward. In 1994 I moved to Phoenix, joining the faculty at Arizona State University West. I was fifty-three. You'd think the life of a university professor would be serene, but the pressure was on us to publish our research. Ph.D. stress had taken its toll, and arriving in Phoenix, I was subject to panic attacks. The first year I didn't publish anything. All I could do was teach my classes and return to my apartment. I had no thought of family or friends, only survival.

I'd been in Phoenix four or five years when David Thomas came to live with me. After many years, I renewed my close contacts with Mary Dorothy. Their father had died. David couldn't care for his sister, so I tried to take up the slack where I could. Summers and holidays when I returned to Texas to visit Kiss and her family, I would sometimes stop for Mary Dorothy, who had moved into a group home in Athens, Texas, a few years earlier.

Ironically, the family Mary Dorothy lived with in Athens was also named Mitchell. I don't know if that caused her obsession with names, but she became Miss Family Tree. When she met someone new, she asked a thousand questions about their background and compared it, and them, to people she knew. Occasionally she stopped strangers in Walmart and asked them their name and who they were kin to.

We grew older. To quote her, we were in our "fives."

Once I stopped to collect Mary Dorothy on my way to Kiss's house. I had just arrived from Phoenix on a Christmas Eve red-eye flight very early in the morning. She was ready for me. When we started to back out of the driveway, she began.

"Liz, Liz, I have an idea, Liz." She said this several times, but I was busy trying to stay out of a deep ditch on either side of the drive.

Finally, to stop the repetition, I braked and said, "What?"

"Let's get some ice cream!" she said. "Good idea, huh Liz?"

"Mary Dorothy, it's 7:15 A.M. on the coldest day of the year. No ice cream."

"Liz, I have another idea. Let's get some pudding."

Obviously, her sweet tooth was demanding attention. I told her no stores were open so early on Christmas Eve. And besides, we were out in the country; there were no stores, period. We rode in silence the 50 or so miles to Kiss's house.

When we arrived, horses surrounded the car. I've always been terrified of huge animals, so I listened for Kiss to tell Benji to go out and shoo the horses away from the car. They were like dogs! They loved the family and thought people in cars carried apples or carrots for them to snack on.

Mary Dorothy had many orthopedic problems which made her unstable on her feet. Benji and I got her inside and I returned to the car to retrieve Christmas presents and suitcases. Mary Dorothy had a shoulder bag of books with her when she entered the house.

After emptying the car, I joined Kiss in the kitchen. She was stirring something on the stove, and when I asked what she was making, she said, "Pudding." That's the thing about Kiss: She was always so sweet to Mary Dorothy.

The next morning when I staggered downstairs to get a cup of coffee, Mary Dorothy was dressed and waiting for someone to get up. I greeted her with a sleepy, "Good morning."

She said, "I want biscuits and gravy and eggs and sausage."

"We're having cereal," I said, pouring a cup of coffee. I went back upstairs to get dressed, and when I returned to the kitchen later, Kiss was cooking biscuits, gravy, eggs, and sausage.

On one of those trips back to Texas, I took Mary Dorothy to Galveston to visit with Lou Lou. They hadn't seen each other in many years. We rode down the seawall, stopped for fresh seafood, crossed the Bay to Bolivar peninsula on the ferry, and did all the other touristy things. It was a good trip. When we weren't out sightseeing, Mary Dorothy quietly read her book.

Back in Phoenix with David Thomas, I was able to report on Mary Dorothy firsthand. She was in good health, despite a hole in her heart and severe hip problems. She needed help with difficult movements, like walking on the uneven ground into Kiss's house. For the most part, she was independent. She could bathe herself, change her clothes, brush her teeth, and perform other personal hygiene tasks. She knew what she liked to eat – mainly hamburgers, Cokes, French fries, and ice cream.

Mary Dorothy was a pleasure to have around most of the time, but when she drank soft drinks, she burped incessantly. Loud, long, and nauseating burps. Toward the end, when I couldn't make her stop, I refused to buy her soft drinks, insisting I didn't want to listen to it.

Her obsession with actors faded, but she was still a reader. Around her neck, she hung her cloth satchel containing about five big, heavy paperback books. If we went to the grocery store, she had her books with her. And she read them every chance she got. I wasn't sure how much of the books she could comprehend because she didn't discuss them with me. When I asked about the stories or plots, she just looked at me like most people look at English teachers. I got the impression the books were personal to her, and she refused to share them with me. When I suggested leaving the books at home while we took short trips to Walmart, she ignored me.

A question crossed my mind as I watched her hang her heavy bag on her shoulder when we left the house: What is *my* bag of books? What do I carry around with me for no good reason weighing me down, making my life more difficult? Maybe character defects like resentments and unforgiveness go with me daily.

One night when she was about sixty-three, she got mad because I wouldn't give her a Coke. She sat on the couch and pouted. After a short time, she looked up at me.

"I love you, anyway," she said. "You're my cousin and I have to love you."

"Well, I love you anyway, too," I said.

On one of our weekends together, I collected Mary Dorothy and her books and took her on a pilgrimage of sorts to visit other members of the family. From Athens, we drove two hours to Mineola to visit my mother's cousin Coulter Templeton. He and his wife had lunch ready for us. From there we drove another two hours to Marshall to the home where Mary Dorothy had grown up. Her father had passed away years before, and we visited with her stepbrother and his housekeeper. Arriving home late in the evening, it was time for bed; I was, as they say on British television, "knackered."

The guestroom bed was higher than usual because of a new mattress. Mary Dorothy said it was too high and she couldn't get on it. I went to get a step stool, but she couldn't climb the steps. Optimistically retrieving another stool, I hoped she could negotiate it, but she was close to hysteria, saying it was too high, too high. The veins on my neck protruded like pencils.

Finally, I said, "Mary Dorothy, take your blanket and pillow and sleep on the couch in the living room. As for me, I have to go to bed." The next morning, I found her asleep in the high bed.

Toward the end of her life, Mary Dorothy developed Alzheimer's disease. She was frightened, she told Mrs. Mitchell, because the pictures on the wall were talking to her. She regressed in her self-care and became more difficult to deal with. Her caregiver and the State of Texas moved her into a memory care facility in Athens. I visited her there, sharing old photos I had of the family, my parents and hers. In the late afternoon, I stood up and said I had to go.

"Sit down," she said. I reminded her I was 67 and didn't like to drive in the East Texas hills after dark.

"I SAID SIT DOWN!" she commanded. I had to laugh. It was so typical of her. She and I had argued back and forth all our lives.

"Hey!" I said. "I didn't even mind my mother; why would you think I'd mind you?" I loved her deeply, my childhood companion, my little charge.

Mary Dorothy died at 65, two years after her brother. I am still amazed this fragile person outlived the others in her immediate family. Kiss and I buried her in Marshall between her mother and father. The chapel was full of people who loved her. A pink marble marker said, "Mary Dorothy Mitchell, beloved daughter."

DAVID THOMAS MITCHELL

David Thomas Mitchell was seventeen when his mother died of breast cancer. His sister Mary Dorothy was nineteen. His father, David Emmitt Mitchell, my mother's brother, was a contractor who built many of the roads in East Texas. From the time David Thomas was about ten, he went to work with his father all summer throughout the eastern part of the state. By fifteen, he was running his own crews in road construction under his father's watchful supervision. At seventeen, David wanted to major in history at Texas A & M, but his father said no.

Uncle David required an engineering degree; therefore, David Thomas, grief-stricken over the loss of his mother, enrolled as a freshman mechanical engineering major. His first college foray didn't last very long. Sometime in the fall, David and some friends got drunk and egged the president's house, leading to his expulsion.

Back home in Marshall, his father got a call from the draft board. David's number was coming up. Chastened by his recent punishment, he quickly joined the Navy, Construction Battalion. Those are the sailors who build roads and prepare for invasion.

I didn't hear from David until he returned from Viet Nam after the war. He finished his engineering degree and married a ballet instructor. As I said before, my life was swallowing me in the '60s, so my mind was not on my family.

One day in 1985, my mama told me David Thomas was missing.

"Missing?" I said.

"Missing!"

No one knew anything. Uncle David hadn't heard from him in over a year. Then it was two years. We were all confused, not knowing whether to be angry at him for neglecting his father or grieved at the thought he could be dead.

On a visit to Marshall, I asked Uncle David about it. "Are you done with him after he's dropped out of our lives?"

"No," he said. "He's my son and I love him."

We didn't hear anything for several more years. In the mid-1990s, David resurfaced back in Marshall, suffering from raging diabetes. I began calling him when he was first hospitalized. He later said he had a breakdown of sorts after his divorce. His experiences in the war, the breakup of his marriage, and daily life in general were too much for him to cope with. Almost paralyzed with depression, he stayed with a friend in Lake Charles, Louisiana, who pulled him back from the darkness while they fished in the Gulf of Mexico.

For a couple of years, David rejoined the family in Texas. In the Shreveport, Veteran's Administration Hospital, doctors amputated his big toe. A few months later, he surprised me in Phoenix with a visit. Back at work, he was building a road through one of the Native American reservations north of Tucson.

Several months later, I learned he was back in the hospital in Shreveport. Doctors amputated his right foot. Then his leg below the knee. Then, after a fall, the leg above the knee. The family watched with horror as this once 6'4" man was reduced to a wheelchair. However, David was surprisingly upbeat about his condition.

"I did it to myself," he said. "I didn't eat right, didn't get medical attention. I have only myself to blame."

Shortly after the last surgery, Uncle David died of a heart attack. David Thomas was released from the hospital for a couple of days to attend his father's funeral. I was in Phoenix and couldn't get away, but Kiss went to Marshall and helped him. He'd lost weight and needed new clothes. She went shopping for him and then helped him get dressed. After the funeral he went back to Shreveport to recover.

In the VA Hospital, David lost his sight. I went to Texas to get him. My home in Phoenix was big enough for both of us, no steps or stairs anywhere, tile floors, open floorplan. It was so much better for him than his late father's carpeted, densely furnished house. I think his stepbrother and the housekeeper were sad to see him leave for Phoenix, but, as I told David, "I need you close where I can keep an eye on you." I wondered whether the narcotics traffickers would murder both of us in Phoenix, but he convinced me the danger was over.

Although he was blind, David Thomas settled into life in Phoenix well. For one thing, he was neater than I was. I think in the Navy he'd learned to make his bed and keep his things in place. The Saltillo tile on the floor was perfect for maneuvering a wheelchair. The bathroom was barely accessible to him, but he made it work. And he could cook. He fixed his own breakfast and lunch; when I returned from work, we usually ate dinner together.

We transferred David's records and filled out new Do Not Resuscitate and living-will forms at the VA Hospital in Phoenix. There was no ophthalmology department there. Our hearts sank until the social worker said, "But we contract with the Mayo Clinic." Over the course of a few months, Mayo doctors in Scottsdale restored David's sight to about forty percent. His quality of life improved greatly.

During the next several years, David shared a few war stories with me. At first, he was reticent, but after a while he began to describe his less horrifying experiences. The first day on the ground in Viet Nam, a helicopter left him at an unmanned outpost. Alone at the makeshift airstrip, he could hear artillery. I asked if he was scared; he replied, "More curious."

"What did you do?"

"I changed out of my dress whites and waited for someone to come get me. I only waited about thirty minutes."

In his description, he said, "Every place has a smell." I wanted him to write about Viet Nam because his stories were beautiful oral narratives, his memories vivid and compelling.

On one patrol, David got separated from American forces in Laos. He led a group into a forest where a sniper killed the others, one by one. David knew if he turned back to the American sector, the sniper would get him, too.

I said, "What did you do?"

"I threw away all my weapons, except my knife," he said. "If the enemy sees you with weapons, it's all over before it begins."

He continued into the forest fifty-three nights, following a river and sleeping during the day until he crossed the border and found an American outpost. "I stole food from homes and drank water from the river. I couldn't ask for help because I didn't know who I could trust."

At the end of his fifty-two-day journey, he walked out of the forest, hands held high, shouting in English to the Americans in the outpost not to shoot him. His hair had grown long, his beard down to his chest.

David became a narc with the CIA when he built a road in her kingdom for the Queen of Thailand, reporting on traffic on the new road. Later, he continued in special operations. His group of trainees were given an order to hide and not be found. The next day, he reported to duty as usual.

"Where the hell have you been?" they demanded.

"Across the street," he replied. He had been the only one to think of leaving the premises while the others were being rounded up. "I figured in war, there weren't many rules."

Connor, I could have these events out of sequence; my information came to me in stories told over a period of years.

David learned enough Thai to get along. He embraced the food and the people. A survivor against all odds, he and his buddy Kirk were hitching a ride in the back of a transport plane when it crashed, bumping and skidding to a halt. One of only two passengers, David said they took about five seconds to exit the plane. Immediately, the pilot and copilot jumped on the emergency chute and landed on top of them. The pilot had managed to land on a narrow road circling a mountain, a deep cliff on one side. They pushed the crashed plane over the cliff and waited for a helicopter to collect them.

In another incident, David and Kirk were traveling in a two-boat convoy on the Mekong River late one night under cover of darkness. They and their captain were in the second boat, which was suddenly blown out from under them. In the river, David realized he wasn't hurt, but the captain had a broken leg. Kirk was nowhere to be found. David pulled the captain to the bank of the river and then swam across to look for Kirk.

"All of a sudden," he said, "I heard gunfire and Kirk yelling, 'Come get me, you sonsabitches! I'm ready for you.'"

David followed Kirk's voice to locate him. Then he heard footsteps behind him.

"I stepped off the path," he said, "into some tall grass. It was so dark you couldn't see anything. Soon I heard a man approach. Then another. Then another." As each of three enemy soldiers advanced, David dispatched them.

When he could move again, he felt his boot on top of something. Using his knife, he cut along the side, dissecting a snake. He hung part of it on his belt and went to find Kirk. Together they swam back across the river to check on the captain. The first boat returned to pick them out of the water and take them to safety.

The snake was a cobra.

My job at Arizona State University West was not going great when David joined me in the late 1990s. I managed to publish a bare minimum of professional material, but it was far from sufficient to get tenure.

David was a wonderful distraction from the crushing stress I felt on the job. We had a good time buying groceries, exploring Phoenix and surrounding Native American reservations. Here's the thing: most of the time I forgot David couldn't see. Several times, driving in Phoenix, usually about half lost, I said, "David, what does that street sign say?"

"You're asking the blind man to read the street sign?" he said. I didn't always remember he was disabled. Much of the time, he was just my cousin from my childhood.

"In my mind, David," I said, "you have no disability!"

We laughed a lot! One of our favorite entertainments was reading *Hank the Cow Dog* books. I found them in the children's section of the Glendale Library; they were so good we read every *Hank* I could find. On Saturdays we would go look for books, I for children's literature and he for the recorded kind. There was a magnificent hotdog stand outside the library where we could get wonderful sausage sandwiches. It was our special Saturday trip. Then we sometimes rode south to the edge of Phoenix, remarking how the rapidly growing city was encroaching on and eliminating local farms.

At a nonprofit for the blind, David ordered audio recordings from the Library of Congress. They sent him a player and compact discs. He bought a computer and enrolled in special classes for the blind.

He amazed me. In a few months, he was teaching word processing to a group of blind women using an oral language application. At Christmas, he led his class through the process of designing a Christmas card. I encouraged him to get them printed, and this he did right away. When he explained who created the cards, Kinko's printed ten copies of each without charge. They even included envelopes.

Phoenix was the best place for David to live because of excellent services for the handicapped. A door-to-door van picked him up and took him to get groceries, to a ballgame, to the center for the blind, anywhere inside Phoenix city limits. I drove him to his hospital checkups. Every trip was exhausting for him.

Connor, as I write in April of 2022, the pandemic is still raging. We in the U.S. watch what is happening in the East, preparing for the newest outbreak here as Covid-19 travels west. Now Shanghai, China, is in lockdown. Twenty-five million people are confined to their homes to prevent the spread of Covid-19 and all its variants.

Another world virus raises its ugly head: monkey pox.

***

In the spring of 2001, Grand Canyon University contracted with a private company in Shanghai to send a professor to teach conversational English to Chinese, mostly Mandarin, speakers. I told the dean I did not want to go to China. However, at the last minute, the professor who had agreed to go jumped ship to Morocco, leaving the university in the lurch. I reluctantly agreed to four weeks in Shanghai; my students were seventeen years old. Jaime, one of my senior GCU students, accompanied me. She was assigned to teach boys and girls thirteen years old. As it turned out, she should have been assigned the older teens because they had a few more years' background in English and were easier to teach.

This experience is difficult to write about because I didn't want to go, and I didn't enjoy China. I left Mickey Howard with David, and traveled from Phoenix to San Francisco to Tokyo to Shanghai. In transit almost twenty-four hours, when we reached Shanghai, I was ready to head back to Phoenix.

I wasn't expecting the climate to be hotter than Arizona. Each day the report of the temperature was in the 30s centigrade, over 100 degrees Fahrenheit, and the humidity was high. I never mastered my chemistry lesson on how to convert Fahrenheit temps from Centigrade. Suffice it to say, with the humidity, it felt like 200 degrees Fahrenheit in Galveston.

We relinquished our passports at the desk of a dormitory, our home the next four weeks. Fortunately, there was an air conditioner in our room, although a maid turned it off each time we exited. From the window, I could see a park with elders performing Tai Chi early each morning. Parks in Shanghai are scarce.

Our bathroom was not clean. Grime separated the tiles in the floor. Glad I had brought an antiseptic cleaner with me, I also had a big bottle of hand sanitizer, which I squirted on far more than my hands. At meals, Jaime and I put the hand sanitizer between us on the table and used it often.

The tables in the dining room were round, seating about eight people. Dormitory food in the U.S. is often far from delicious; imagine its Chinese counterpart. Every lunch and dinner came to us on dented metal trays, the kind you'd imagine Alcatraz prisoners ate from. There was always a fish serving with the most and the tiniest bones possible. I became quite expert at eating down to and removing the skeleton before finishing the fish. With chopsticks!

Most meals offered boiled shrimp, which would have been great, but they were served heads on, eyes bulging and red "strings" dissecting the adjacent white rice. The Chinese, who never touched their food with their hands, put the whole shrimp in their mouths and chewed and sucked the juice until only the shell remained. Then they spit them out on the plastic tablecloth beside their plates. Jamie and I slathered the hand sanitizer again.

If there were no shrimp, our other protein dish was eels, entirely new to me. Our Chinese teacher's aide, displaying a drooping black eel between her chopsticks, said, "Seafood. When the menu says seafood, they give you little snakes." I couldn't look at them.

Every meal included a serving of mystery greens. I didn't recognize the variety, but I really liked them. Jaime didn't care for them, so I ate hers, too. The dessert was always the same, a seedless watermelon sliced into individual servings. I learned to eat all the rice to fill myself up. Jaime didn't eat much at all at first, but hunger got to her, and she became more adventuresome.

Portions of everything were small, so I usually left the table hungry.

Next door to the dormitory, there was a convenience store. Inside they sold chips, milk, and Chinese staples. I discovered a to-die-for liquid yogurt. It came in quart containers, and my daily habit grew to a quart a day, sometimes two, depending on how hungry I was. I'm sure it was made with whole milk and very fattening, so I was surprised when I lost eight pounds in China.

One day we arrived for lunch as the bus person was clearing our table. I watched him use a grimy gray rag to rake the shrimp shells off the table into a little bucket. Then he wiped the table down with the same rag and went to the next table to do the same. I wondered if the plastic tablecloth had ever been cleaned.

Shanghai has four very different faces. The first is the Chinese skyline. Gray residence buildings reaching to the sky for miles. The apartments inside reminded me of a rabbit warren. Small, cluttered, and claustrophobic. Then there's the Chinese street scene. Bicycles, rickshaws, taxis, and other automobiles weaving around each other, dodging pedestrians and passing among sidewalk businesses where people cooked their meals outside their stores.

The other two sectors refer to architecture. The German sector appears as great stone institutions on one side of the river, the site of banks and other commercial ventures from an earlier time. On the other side, a modern city rose, the Pudong, as if overnight. These buildings are futuristic: a round building with a map of the world on its exterior, triangular structures, and tall towers.

Toward the end of our month, our boss took us to an exclusive restaurant in the Pudong section of the city. Walking to our table, we passed a waiter putting dishes on a table. The smell was the worst I'd ever experienced. Once we were seated, we remarked to each other about it. One of the men in our party overheard us and said it wasn't the waiter smelling so bad; it was the dish he was serving.

"It's called 'Capitalism,'" he said. "Smells so bad but tastes so good."

Jaime ate a bite of it. I refused. She said it was bad.

Our dormitory was situated down the block from an internet "café." For just a few pennies, I could spend my lunch hour on the internet trying to connect with someone in the U.S. I got through only to a friend in Kansas. My messages were usually, "I'm dyin' over here. Talk to me, Barbara." We were able to reminisce about the past; it was a little bit of sanity in the crazy situation I found myself in.

The students were the best part of our experience. After a few days, I realized that there was little difference teaching Chinese kids, except they were respectful and socially less jaded than American teens. I believe their home culture contributed to both conditions. They weren't allowed to date or have special friends, and their days were packed from 5:30AM to midnight with music and/or sports lessons, school, and studying.

Chinese women were required to retire at age 60, men at 65. They lived with their adult child who supported them completely and depended on them for child supervision. There was only one child allowed each couple. A child's parents are strict, sometimes to the point of being abusive. I guess the parents wanted the child to grow into a good wage earner because they would be dependent on him/her for support. One of my students arrived in class one morning, put her head on her desk and sobbed. I knelt by her desk and asked if she was all right.

"My mother beat me today," she said.

"Was it bad?" I asked.

"Yes."

"I'm so sorry." In the U.S., I would be required to report the incident, but in China, it was often business as usual. I learned volumes from teaching Chinese children.

The absence of churches was one of my first impressions of China. In Mixon, Texas, population of just a couple hundred people, there are no stores but two churches, and in Jacksonville, population fourteen thousand, there are various Christian churches all over town. Jaime and I looked for one in Shanghai but saw none. Finally, she asked her students if there was a Christian church anywhere in town.

A student named a Catholic church across this city of twenty million people, writing the Chinese characters for the location of the church and the return to the dormitory on a slip of paper. One early Sunday morning, we ventured out of the dorm and hailed a taxi. The driver read the student's note and drove and drove and drove, dodging other taxis, bicyclists, shoppers, and others. At the end of this journey, we found ourselves in front of a huge old Western-style building. Inside we followed the crowd upstairs and found a seat in a huge auditorium. The congregation looked to be over a thousand people.

The music was a surprise. It sounded like the old hymns we Methodists sang when I was a child: "Rock of Ages," "Just as I Am," and others. The surprise for me was how the songs sounded in Chinese. The church filled to the rafters, and girls in white dresses and boys in dressy attire filed down to the altar for their first communion. Parents were taking pictures, so I took pictures, too. Although I am not Catholic, I could almost follow the Chinese liturgy: the first reading, the Gospel reading, the prayer of confession, and so on. At the end of the service, everyone went to the back and filed down the center aisle where the priest pressed the Host into their hands.

When I could see the end of the line, I stood and told Jaime I was going to join them. She said, "I'm not Catholic."

"Neither am I," I said, "but I just want to touch the hem of His garment." It was the closest I'd been to Christian fellowship in two weeks. Students said later this church was the largest Christian church in China.

I was last in line. In front of the priest, I held out my hands like the Episcopalian I am. He must have noticed my pink skin because when he placed the Host in my hand, he said in English,

"The body of Christ!" It felt so good. I was refreshed and sure I could hold out two more weeks in this foreign environment.

Children in China are like children everywhere; but their education is vastly different. They pay utmost respect to the teacher, standing when they are called on. As lovely as this sounds, it was difficult to run conversational questions past them. To teach them to think in English, I pointed to individuals and asked questions like, "What did you have for breakfast?" If I didn't receive an immediate answer, I moved to the next student in the circle, "What color is your shirt?" Standing was a way to buy some time for students to translate from Mandarin to English.

Chinese students learned English from Chinese teachers and British audio programs. Their pronunciation of some sounds was decidedly British, such as *cahn't* for *can't*. Children began the study of English at primary level, choosing an English name for themselves along the way. I taught some Sherrys and Daniels; Jaime had one named Table. My most unusual was a boy named Sonic. Compared to American teens, they were a young seventeen years. My favorite student was a boy named Charles Wilson.

Charles wore short pants with a shirt buttoned to his neck every day. Even better behaved than most of the other students, he tried harder with the pronunciation of difficult sounds. He found it impossible to say /th/, substituting /z/ in words like mother, father, and brother. After a long time of mozzer, fazzer, and brozzer, Charles said in frustration, "I cahn't due it!"

"Yes, you can!" I said. "Look at my tongue when I say it. Put your tongue under your upper teeth." But he really couldn't "due" it.

In the Chinese classroom, getting the right answer was of utmost importance. When I asked a question, the answer became a group project. When I tried to restrict the solution to one student only, the result was whispered aid. They could not understand plagiarism. I had to solve this problem by asking questions only one student could answer. And if I gave them something to read, they memorized it. After watching a pirated version of *Spiderman*, I called ten students to the front of the room, asking the first in line for the first development in the plot sequence. Then the second student told what happened next, and down the line to the end of the story. This worked well because [a] students were already standing and couldn't stall for time, and [b] they didn't know ahead of time what the previous student's answer was to be. At the end of the month, one student wrote in my Goodbye Book, "Thank you, Doc Ho. When I started your class, I couldn't speak English. Now I can."

Everywhere we went, crowds made it difficult to navigate – even the little convenience store next door had a long line of people waiting to check out. The boss took us on a weekend trip to Beijing. We stayed at a beautiful five-star hotel Friday night and spent Saturday sightseeing.

After talking to some English-speaking Chinese people, Jaime and I often went into a quick conference to try to figure out what they were saying. Our first stop was something our [English-speaking] guide called "the serteenst mingtoo." Immediately Jaime and I went into a huddle to try to decipher the message, to no avail. It turns out he was saying, "The thirteenth Ming tomb." He failed to tell us about the other twelve Ming tombs, or what the significance of this experience was. We walked up a flight of concrete steps to a courtyard and then down several flights to a big room underground. Of course, there were crowds of people on the courtyard, the stairs, and in the tomb. When we got down to the room at the bottom of the stairs, we saw a huge red box and were told we were looking at the casket of the thirteenth Ming ruler.

Jaime was incensed. "That's it?" she said. "We walked all this hot way to see a red box?"

Outside in the courtyard we were ushered into a souvenir shop. Jim, the other professor from GCU, showed me a small red silk pillowcase with a picture embroidered on it. "It's a Chinese legend, the grandfather with 100 grandchildren," he said proudly. "I got it for 35 yuan."

I went over to look at them and chose a larger one. Then I talked the salesperson down to 35 yuan. Couldn't wait to say, "Mine's bigger than yours!"

The boss approached with three green popsicles to mitigate the baking heat. The three of us Americans grabbed them with all the gusto of a dying Saharan traveler grabbing a drink of water. Expecting a sweet lime flavor, I experienced the taste of pea soup. Almost gagging, Jaime and I threw the nasty stuff in the trash. Jim, on the other hand, ate the whole thing.

At Tiananmen Square, a huge cement space across the street from the Forbidden City, Jaime and I stayed in the airconditioned bus and looked out the windows at a huge crowd of people on a concrete parking lot. Later, inside the huge walls around it, we entered the Forbidden City through the Gate of Divine Might. A colorful brochure reported over 900 palaces, furnished with ornate lacquered tables and chairs. We stood outside plexiglass doors to ooh and ahh over the splendor in a couple of rooms before I lost interest. I stood behind about 100 people and didn't see much more than the backs of their heads. The Chinese are desperate for something to look at. Crowds everywhere! Even where there is nothing to see like in Tiananmen Square.

On our way out, we found some shade. Cooling a bit on some stone steps, we greeted a small group of Americans passing by. They stopped for a short visit and introduced themselves. They were from Marshall, Texas, and knew my uncle David. It's time to say, "Small world."

Next stop was the Great Wall at Badaling. Did I mention it was hot? There were millions of steps getting up to the wall, then millions going to the top of the wall. Jim invited me to walk to the top with him.

"I'm going to wait till I get back to Phoenix to have my heart attack," I said.

Undaunted, he started up the long climb. Once at the top, he waved to me and then started back down, in reverse. People going up couldn't help staring at him, but still he continued down the steps backwards. When he got to the bottom, he said his leg muscles cramped at the top of the wall and wouldn't permit him to descend properly.

The next attraction was the summer palace. This was something to see! It looked like a barge of white marble at the edge of a lake. Walking out on it, I understood why the empress lived there in the summertime. The marble in water created a cooler atmosphere.

On Sunday morning, we had breakfast in the hotel before leaving for the airport. The pea soup popsicle had given Jim dysentery.

The trip from Beijing to Shanghai was a nightmare. When we boarded the plane in the evening, a storm was about to strike our area. We sat on the hot plane over four hours, deafened by loud thunder and terrified by rocking back and forth from the wind. People in the plane were starting to mutiny, raising all kinds of protests, asking to return to the terminal. However, the terminal wasn't connected to the plane by a passageway. We would have had to exit the plane in the storm and walk to the terminal. I was relieved to take my chances inside the plane.

Our flight landed in Shanghai about 2:30 A.M. Jaime and I went back to the dormitory in a taxi. As the driver left us at the front door, we discovered in the dark a padlocked chain around the door handles, locking us out and everyone else in. We made a lot of noise until someone from the inside unlocked the chain and let us in. It was 3:45 A.M. I was afraid of fire consuming us since we were padlocked inside every night.

The trip back to Phoenix was blissfully uneventful, except the travel arrangements involved a ten-hour layover in San Francisco. Ankles swollen to the size of tree trunks, I joined Jaime in a visit to Fisherman's Wharf and a fresh fish lunch. Back at the airport, we waited. The airline offered to drive us to

San Jose to catch an earlier plane to Phoenix. I jumped at the chance.

Back home in Phoenix, I greeted David and slept three days.

A Failing Giant of a Man

David's health slowly deteriorated to a serious degree. His kidneys were not functioning properly; his diabetes demanded the constant discipline of eating right and medications. It was difficult for me to see him begin to fail. However, his attitude and mood remained good. I was the one who got depressed.

I had a close friend in Phoenix named Colleen, a professional photographer, a shooter of society weddings. One day she called when I wasn't home and talked to David. They began a friendship lasting the rest of his life. She spoke to him daily over several years.

Every Thursday when Dave the pool man arrived, David wheeled out to the pool to talk to him, telling fish stories. Dave had a boat, and occasionally he took David to the lake for overnight fishing trips.

Denied tenure at ASUW, I joined the faculty at Grand Canyon University as an associate professor of reading education. My life became busier than usual. However, relieved of the pressure to publish, I produced more there than I had before.

David's health continued to deteriorate. At one point, he was hospitalized and then placed in a nursing home for rehabilitation. He stayed there three months, hating every minute of it. I tried to cheer him up, providing him with all the gossip from the university and occasionally gifting him with something he asked for, like a hamburger. I wasn't worried that he was critically ill, but I should have been. He called one morning and said the paramedics were coming to take him to the hospital because he couldn't stop vomiting. I said, "I'll be right there."

I arrived as the emergency personnel were wheeling him out on a stretcher; at the hospital, we sat in a newly painted space downstairs, waiting for a regular hospital room. There were no monitors, oxygen connections, television. Not even a telephone. As he lay asleep on the hospital bed, I read on my Kindle. At noon, I said I was going home to eat lunch, but I would return shortly.

An hour later, I returned to find him the same. He was awake, but his eyes were closed. I had been reading just a few minutes when he sat straight up in the bed and said, "I feel lightheaded." Then he fell back on the pillow.

I said, "David, you're scaring me." When I found him unresponsive, I screamed. Running out into the hall, I continued to scream. I couldn't even think. People came running!

After only a minute or two, they wheeled equipment into the room; I heard the doctor say, "Clear!" Standing in the hall just outside the door, I had stopped screaming, but sobs wracked my body. A secretary came out of her office and asked if I wanted to go sit down. I just shook my head.

Almost immediately, the crisis ended. Several people rolled David's bed out into the hall and into an elevator. The doctor was barking orders to them. The scene was chaotic.

Catching up to the doctor, I said, "He has a Do Not Resuscitate."

"Well, we just resuscitated him," he said.

Later at home, I was still crying. Afraid David would be angry with me, I had forgotten about his DNR! Sobbing, I called my list of family and friends to tell them what happened: David had a heart attack, but the hospital personnel had brought him back. I choked out the information to about a dozen people, my daughter Kiss, cousins, and friends. I will be forever grateful to David's lifelong friend, Jim Harris, a physician in Marshall.

"You did the right thing, Elizabeth," Jim said. "The DNR is for when he has no chance to recover." Relieved, I stopped crying.

In 2003 I retired from Grand Canyon University although I stayed online with them in their master's program in education. My income declined some, and I feared I would have to return to Texas because of affordability. But what about David? We began to look for a place for him. When he found an apartment a few miles away, Dave the pool man helped him move his things.

Shake My Hand

Connor, when I retired from Grand Canyon University, Arizona had only one public high school for adjudicated teens. Students in the school weren't judged and found guilty of specific crimes; the only judgment was "incorrigible, based on a pattern of criminality." A boy could do several years behind the razor wire at Adobe Mountain for theft of a bicycle if he had a history of appearing in court. The sentences lasted to the child's eighteenth birthday.

In 2003, three boys hanged themselves at Adobe Mountain. Two of them had previously expressed suicidal ideation; the third had attempted to kill himself in the past. Deciding to detour around retirement, I applied for and accepted a reading/language arts teacher position for the 2003-2004 school year and prepared myself for a year of discovery. I felt compelled to learn about conditions at the school, the content of the curriculum, the boys themselves, and whether a teacher could make a lasting difference in broken children.

Located on the north side of Phoenix, Adobe Mountain School couldn't decide whether they were a prison containing a school or a school located inside a prison, as revealed in the way they treated the students and teachers. I hope things have changed significantly since then.

On July 7, my first day on the job, I approached the sally gate right on time, 7:45. Lynet, a new math teacher, and some others stood around outside the gate. We all entered at the same time, some going for the sign-in book. Lynet and I emptied our purses into plastic tubs for Security to inspect. The guard, a scowling Hispanic woman named Mariselli, paused over my book bag to tell me Kevin, the principal, wanted to see us both.

Outside the Admin Building, Kevin, tall and shaped like a bowling pin in a wilted cheap suit, wiped sweat from his face with a handkerchief and told us to substitute for Ms. Tarnower, an English teacher absent for the day. I looked to Lynet for leadership because she had been on the job two whole weeks.

We entered the classroom as about fifteen boys dressed in yellow tee shirts and blue jeans arrived and slouched into desks arranged in a circle. They looked well-scrubbed and wouldn't have appeared out of place in any public high school. Teenage boys don't have much in the way of hips, and they weren't allowed a belt; therefore, many of them relied on the way they moved around the room to avoid losing their pants.

One student approached me and said, "Shake my hand." I didn't usually touch students until I knew them, but when he held his hand out to me, I shook it. He sat in about the nine o'clock position in the circle and opened the book on his desk.

Mrs. Tarnower had left instructions for the class to read a short story about homophobia. An interesting tale about a boy from a broken home who went to live with an uncle and his gay friend, the story was well crafted and should have captivated the class, but Lynet set them to reading round-robin style. The boys' plodding lack of fluency destroyed the intent of the lesson. I stopped the reading and asked questions.

"What do we know about this person? What is his situation?"

I looked over at Mr. Shake My Hand. Both his hands were stuck down into the front of his jeans in what could only have been masturbation.

"Stop!" I said in my best teacher voice. "Put your hands on your desk." I was surprised he obeyed. None of the other boys visibly noticed this bit of drama.

I resumed reading the story to the boys. They became more responsive to the characters, and things were moving satisfactorily when Mr. Shake did it again. This time, he had one hand around his throat choking himself, his face a neon scarlet. *Jesus help me!* Again, I stopped him, then continued the reading.

We almost finished the story before the end of class, and as the boys left the room, only one asked if he could take the book to continue to read. Lynet said the boys weren't allowed to have books in their cells. I wondered, "What kind of school doesn't allow books?"

As the students left the classroom with their youth correction officers (YCOs), I was glad I had brought a large bottle of hand sanitizer. In the hall, I heard Lynet say, "I'm not going to shake your hand! Get out of here! Yuck!"

Death Row

By 2003, I had well over thirty-five years' teaching experience and a master's and Ph.D. in teaching English language acquisition. Not expecting many new insights into the practice of teaching, I planned to learn about *these* boys and *this* school, specifically.

Like the Chinese tourists I saw in Beijing, boys at Adobe Mountain proved desperate to find something of interest in their daily lives. Tiananmen Square is a huge concrete slab, a parking lot with no cars. Yet there were thousands of people milling around, showing their babies and children "the sights." There were no sights!

Adobe Mountain cells were bare; television entertainment was limited; no books, paper, or pencils were allowed. The boys anxiously searched for something to see, anything to do. They had nothing else to think about but each other. They reminded me of puppies, jumping on each other and playing in little skirmishes as they learned how to be adults. However, there were few adults willing to teach them how to act. Instead, the students were repeatedly punished for breaking the rules, most of which were so unknown as to be secret. Sometimes their first indication they had done something wrong was their punishment.

I listened to them talk about the guards, about each other, about their classes. Achievement test scores revealed many were reading at the primary level. There were no obvious high achievers at Adobe Mountain, but all my students could speak English. What a relief! Arizona has well over 100 different language communities.

The first group galloped into my classroom and shoved the chairs and tables around to suit themselves. Above the cacophony of scraping furniture on the floor and insulting greetings among the students, I overheard one student tell another, "She better not ask us to read anything!"

Anticipating a dislike of reading, I found a little book in the Glendale Public Library, a dispassionate account of the daily life of Stanley "Tookie" Williams, who had been convicted of four murders and sentenced to death row in San Quentin. I distributed fifteen illegal copies and began reading to all three classes the first day.

At the end of two weeks, my voice was gravelly from overuse. The principal said classes would be re-assigned. I would lose half my students and gain about seven or eight others. Fortunately, after the reshuffle, all the students wanted to read *Life in Prison* from start to finish, the second time around for many of them. The boys devoured the book and joined discussions about the death penalty, "Tookie" Williams' Crips gang, and their own crimes.

The students were well behaved and engaged in the subject matter. They wrote short pieces about similarities and differences between San Quentin and Adobe Mountain. The *New York Times* published an article about Williams, who had been nominated several times for a Nobel Prize for his efforts to encourage young people to be good citizens. The students took this opportunity to write letters to the editor, reporting on the effects Williams' story had on their thinking. Their first efforts were covered with gang tags, but when I insisted the editors would not consider them seriously, they settled down and followed a business-letter format. I sent all the letters to *NYT*.

After San Quentin, we read about homeless people in America. Our text was suffocatingly boring, relating every statistic available about the age and background of homeless people in major U.S. cities. About halfway through the first chapter, we agreed to ditch the text and called upon our own observations of local tent cities, questioning, "Was it the government's job to provide life support for everybody?"

The boys' responses surprised me. Some felt homeless people were lazy, alcoholic, and drug addicted. The others expressed compassion for those born into poverty or suffering tragic life failures. We went through the process of listing pro and con opinions about the government's responsibilities in the matter of homelessness. Each student chose a point of view and wrote a persuasive essay to express his opinion, refuting arguments advanced by those in the class who disagreed with them. Some of their sentences made me laugh: "Some people say homeless people are lazy and sit on their ass instead of working," one student began. "But I feel bad for those who are sick and lost their job." They wrote just like they talked, but their thinking was sound for the most part.

Da Dum

Our whole semester proved to be hard work but productive on everyone's part. Think of teaching a dozen twelve-month-old puppies to sit side by side in a line. Early on, students tried to steal my electric pencil sharpener to create a tattoo machine. I had to get a YCO to lock down my room until the device was miraculously discovered on top of a filing cabinet.

The boys explored every inch of the classroom before they settled down for a lesson. Their language was peppered with f-bombs, which caused me to caution them; they usually said, "Sorry, Miss," before they continued. And they refused to take tests. They registered as non-readers on achievement tests because they wrote their names at the top of the scantron sheet and didn't answer any questions.

I had some pleasant surprises, too. There were no violent incidents in my classroom among rival gangs. The students liked each other. There was only one student I was afraid of, but I felt sure the other boys in the class would protect me from him. His name was Justin, and he was the only Native American among my classes. When he came in late on the first day, I asked him to come to class on time.

"You are only saying that because I'm an Indian," he said in a menacing, aggressive voice.

"No," I said. "it's because you are ten minutes late." He seethed with rage, scaring me away from confronting him again. He was on time the rest of the semester.

Often when my voice cracked after hours of reading aloud, I took a short break and asked for a substitute reader. A volunteer allowed us to continue. They could read just fine! To one boy, I whispered, "You did a good job of reading!"

"I just did what you do," he said, smiling.

When the text related a startling fact, like "Caesar Chavez had eight children when he left for California's fields to pick fruit," the reader stopped the flow of the story to exclaim, "Goddam, Miss!"

I began a unit on poetry with a sonnet from Shakespeare.

The boys were taken by this love poem. They stopped the study of poetry almost before it began and set about writing their own love poems to their girlfriends and, in a couple of cases, their wives. They refused to care that sonnets have fourteen lines. A poem is a poem.

When I introduced the iambic rhythm concept, they politely listened:

Shall I compare thee to a summer's day?
Thou art more temperate...

Da dum da dum da dum da dum da dum. Sympathetic faces silently said, "The old girl has gone over the edge."

They typed their finished poems in a rococo font and illustrated them with crayon flowers and flourishes. Their poems reflected their language; I reminded myself repeatedly, "It's just words."

We read some stories about aliens from space. The youngest boy in the class said, "Miss, you ever think these stories we're reading are bullshit?"

"I'm so glad you spoke up, Tommy." I had been waiting to see how long it would take someone to question the text. I welcomed the first doubts to surface. Here was an opportunity to discuss levels of language and how to substitute good words for bad, especially when you want to show respect. I wrote <u>bullshit = absurd</u> on the board.

"I'm from Texas, and we know bullshit!" I said. "But there is sometimes a more useful word. We discussed the times it would be better to use a "real" word when speaking to someone you didn't want to offend. Like a judge or a cop.

Several times over the next few days, I quizzed the classes, "Class, what does *absurd* mean?" The answer always came in a choral reply of "bullshit!"

"I teach vocabulary!" I explained to the YCO assigned to my classroom.

Then one day a guard chased Miguel into my room. The boy's face was red and panicky. "Miss," he said, "they think I tagged the cafeteria. I didn't do it!"

"He had the marker in his hand," the guard said.

"That's bull..." Miguel stopped and tried to think of his new socially acceptable word. "It's bullsh..." He finally remembered, stood straighter, and smiled as he blurted out, "It's fuckin' absurd!" The guard led him away.

Getting Ready

Employee orientation at Adobe Mountain was a marriage of nightmare and joke. I began my term in a two-week period between three-month terms. I thought I had time to prepare, but most of those days were spent downtown in the required Academy, the Arizona Department of Juvenile Corrections (ADJC). There, all the newbies were instructed on a brain-bludgeoning history of ADJC, some confusing philosophy-of-corrections lectures, cardio-pulmonary resuscitation training, and legal issues.

The pretty young leader of the legal issues seminar misspelled words and pretty much jumbled her presentation. In her list of topics to cover, she listed *consaquences* (sic). At one point, she cited the case of Jones v. Mitsubishi. Jones tried to hold the car company responsible for his carpal tunnel, which, he insisted, was caused by working on the assembly line. She announced the verdict: "The decision of the Court? Jones lost and Mr. Bishi (sic) won."

Back in Esperanza Building classroom 13 on the Adobe Mountain campus, I could not learn anything useful. At the first staff meeting, a poster met us as we entered the auditorium, announcing the topic: perseverance. Somehow Kevin misread the sign as "preservation," and spent about fifteen minutes lecturing us on taking care of school property. When he discovered his error, he turned the meeting over to an assistant principal and left. Clueless in this cloud of nonsense, I tried to plan classes. While the boys were due to appear in my classroom in three days, I still had no texts, no desks, and no idea what I would greet when they arrived.

After the meeting, a new assistant principal wandered into my classroom. Great! I had some questions:

"How can I order some materials to teach with?" I asked.

"Give me a list," he said.

"I don't have enough desks and chairs," I said.

"Go find some."

"Where?"

"Look in the book room," he said.

"Nothing in my classroom locks. Where can I get keys?"

"Security, I think, but I'm not sure."

Suspended in uncertainty, I gave the assistant principal a list of ten classroom sets of young adult novels. He put the list in his pocket then exited the room, and I never saw him or the list again.

By the start of classes, I scrounged twelve desks and chairs, arranged them in the tiny room, and taped some colorful book jackets on the wall. Jose Canito was the first student to enter.

Small and pleasant and smiling big, he said, "I'm in your class." Throughout the semester, I observed Jose spend his time in class drawing cartoon characters: Mickey Mouse, Porky Pig, and others. He knew where I had a stash of crayons and collected them upon entering the room. I had to admit, the pictures were good, and throughout the semester, they filled a notebook. Jose continued to be the first student to show up for class and always greeted me with, "Hey, Girl!"

Other students left all kinds of drawings in my classroom, from people to marijuana plants. Sometimes they put them on my desk as they exited the room; other times they left them on the floor. None were X-rated.

Jose Canito took it upon himself to teach me how to pronounce his last name. "When you say it, Miss, it hurts." I was pronouncing Canito with a /t/ that was obviously offensive to Jose. We went through a little lesson several times where he tried to get me to pronounce the /t/ like /tth/, /Caneet-though/.

"I'm sorry, Jose," I said, "but I'm from Texas, and I talk funny."

There was a day when we were reading *Life in Prison* and discussing their arrests. I chanted the line from the "Cops" television program: "Bad boys, bad boys, whatcha gonna do when they come for you?"

Someone said, "They already came for us!"

Another student said, "Look where we are!" By this time several boys were laughing.

I asked, "How many of you were under the influence of alcohol or drugs when you were arrested?"

All but Jose raised a hand. "They came for me at six o'clock in the morning," he said, pleased, "and I was still asleep."

Jose and Luis

Jose Ortega, a bright seventeen-year-old, somehow convinced someone in the principal's office he needed two classes of English rather than one. He entered on the first day and found a seat in front of one of the two functional computers, saying he wanted to work on his exit papers.

While the class studied and discussed *Life in Prison*, Jose taught himself word processing. Refusing my help with punctuation and capitalization, he studied a printed page from one of our stories and learned both quite successfully. At the end of each class, he put the printed version on my desk and asked for a notebook to bind his "stories."

In his short life Jose had been ejected from his home by his parents, joined a gang, gotten married, and fathered a baby girl. He was, he said, in Adobe Mountain for a variety of minor scrapes with the law. His last offense was bicycle theft. He admitted to being jealous and threatening violence to his wife, who had left the relationship and returned to her parents.

One Wednesday in the middle of the semester, Jose arrived in class, face flushed and obviously lethargic. I could see he was sick but was unable to get help for him because, as staff informed me, boys weren't allowed back in their cottage until the end of the school day. There was a nurse on campus, but Jose refused to go see her.

"I'll just stay here with you," he said.

After a couple of hours leaning against the desk and computer, Jose made his way to the floor, saying he just needed to rest. He was hot to the touch and lethargic, headachy, his red grimace displaying discomfort. The only place he could lie on the floor without being stepped on was under my desk, so he spent three days' class time sleeping there, returning to his cottage at the end of the day. About every hour, I left the classroom – illegally – to fill my little water bottle with cold water from the teachers' fountain. Insisting he drink it, I was doing the only thing I was allowed to do for him. Staff I talked to about him were unconcerned.

On Monday, Jose returned to class feeling better, took up his position at the computer, and resumed work on his memoirs. I learned from another student while I was out of the room, the boys sat quietly, surprised and touched by my kindness to Jose.

While Jose believed he knew everything going on, Luis Balboa was the opposite. A pleasant sixteen-year-old, Luis arrived on time and participated in the activities of the day. When asked a question about anything, Luis' stock answer was, "I have no idea."

"Luis, what story were we reading?"

"I have no idea." No idea of the date, the time, where someone was, who the hero of the story was. No idea, whatever the question.

As the class eagerly – and prematurely – settled down to write their love poems, Luis was focused. Brow furrowed, he labored over his poem, erasing occasionally. Before the end of the class, he brought his paper for me to admire. One day he had seen his girlfriend walking by and fallen in love at first sight. They started to date and then got serious. His last line brought me up short: *Sweetheart/I love you and/I think of you every fucking day.*

I almost laughed out loud. "Luis, this is beautiful," I said, "but we need to do something about your last sentence."

Discussing again the concept of levels of language, I said the F-bomb was likely to distract from the strong, pure emotion behind his poem.

"What other word can you use instead? Every blank day, every blank, blank, blank day? How else can you say this?"

"I have no idea," he said.

"Take this back to your desk and think," I said.

Luis failed to arrive at a solution to the F-word problem. At the end of class, I suggested the word *single*, "Every single day." Pleased, he wrote it down.

Teacher Morale at ADJC

Teacher morale in Esperanza Building was the lowest I had ever seen. Several of the teachers avoided eye contact when they talked to me. They were expected to be on campus Monday through Friday, even during the three weeks when classes were not in session. Regularly denied earned vacation time during an intercession when no classes met, one of the teachers had won a cruise to Somewhere Great, but she wasn't allowed time off to go.

It was not unusual to require faculty to stay late for special tasks, such as reassigning all the students to different classes. I stayed until 6:00 one evening when the others refused. A new assistant principal, another new teacher, and I placed 150 boys we hadn't met with teachers we didn't know.

After school, professional educators weren't allowed to go to the library and bookstores to locate appropriate curriculum. We had to remain on campus, as another teacher observed, to cover Arizona's backside. While we were onsite, the numbers showed a greater ratio of teachers to students, making the prison/school look better on paper. Paper evidence also showed a low incidence of recidivism, repeat offenders. Another teacher said this was deception, paper magic. If students re-offended after being discharged, upon re-entry they were recorded as repeat offenders only if they were charged with the same crime. Previous bicycle thieves would not qualify as recidivist if they stole something different.

Of the five computers in my classroom only two worked and were not connected to the internet. There were no overhead projectors, audio players, or any other kind of technology available to teachers. We used a whiteboard, markers, and crayons in addition to pencils, which had to be counted before and after each class.

It was hard to get inside the razor wire, to teach our classes with limited resources. Newspapers and magazines were "contraband," according to the guard at the gate, and therefore denied. I couldn't get the *New York Times* past the guard at the gate.

"Contraband!" she said. "No newspapers!"

"This is a New York newspaper, not Phoenix," I argued.

"Contraband," she repeated.

Videos and classical music on CDs were also refused. All incoming materials were searched and approved – or not – by the disagreeable, officious Maricelli at the sally gate. Apparently, this public-school curriculum was determined by a high school graduate who might have gotten through on GED, a test written on the eighth-grade level, the state-mandated curriculum be damned.

One day she told me I had to go home and change clothes because the suit I wore too closely resembled denim.

"It's not denim," I insisted.

"It's the same color," she said.

"Okay," I said, giving up. "But if I go home, I am not coming back. Explain it to the principal if you can." She let me in.

Guards regularly invaded and inspected our classrooms, squawky walkie talkies blaring. What is noteworthy is I couldn't understand a word from them, but the boys listened intently and then discussed what was said from guard to guard over the devices hanging from their belts.

Incarceration became the normal for students and teachers alike. Several boys shared with me they would end up in adult prison because that's where their mothers and fathers were. CYOs were fired on the spot. Teachers were hanging on to their jobs because they had only a few years left before they could retire.

"If I could get another job," one said, "I would go for it."

"If you can teach here," I said, "you can teach anywhere!" They were unconvinced. Demeaned and intimidated, they hunkered down and accepted their "sentences," almost as institutionalized as the inmates. A crisis occurred when I asked for leave during the intercession to go to Baltimore for three days to attend the wedding of Peggy's son.

"Denied," the principal said.

"Why?" I demanded.

"Because we are planning to hold staff development seminars for teachers," he said.

"I have a Ph.D. in English acquisition in public schools," I reminded him. "I lead staff development seminars and know how to teach reading and writing."

"Well, we're going to write a curriculum for the Arizona Juvenile Department of Corrections," he said. "We'll need you." He said *we*. Did he have a mouse in his pocket?

Connor, translate the principal's language into either:

"We won't get around to it, so you won't have to do anything"

or

"Elizabeth, you will rewrite the entire state curriculum for juvenile inmates, and we won't pay you for it."

Feeling the straight jacket of institutionalization close around me, I quit.

The wedding was beautiful!

Full Stop

Jose Ortega made a big impression on his classmates with his printed stories. Many of the boys asked him to help them produce attractive exit papers of their own. I brought several used folders from home to collect the essays in a stack on my desk. Activity around the two working computers increased. Jose assumed the role of instructional technologist for the classroom. Several of the boys taught themselves paragraphing and other editing skills under Jose's tutelage. Soon the collection of exit papers grew.

A visibly distressed Israel Rivera asked me to help him after school. Before a student could be released early, before his eighteenth birthday, he had to jump through some literary hoops by preparing several documents, one of which was a narrative essay about his life including his family background, his troubles with the law, his arrest, and his time at Adobe Mountain. ADJC wanted an explanation of the delinquent behavior and a noticeable amount of remorse. Without the latter, there would be no early release.

"I can't write it, Miss," Israel said, looking scared.

"Why?"

His voice rose on the accented middle of his answer, giving it three syllables instead of two.

"Be-CAU-ause," he explained, "I don't know how. I never wrote nothing before."

"Well, *I* know how. I'll help you if you can get permission to come to my room after school."

Wednesday when the others had returned to their cottages, Israel pulled a desk next to mine and I looked at the instructions for the paper he was to write: a narrative broken into several parts – *my home and family, when I got into trouble, my arrest.*

ADJC was looking for some analytical thinking on the following topics: *What I did wrong, how my actions affected my victim, what I should have done instead, how I can stay out of trouble in the future."*

To his credit, Israel did not tag his paper with his gang sign. He had titled his paper *my life*, which we replaced with the title in the instructions, *Narrative*. At my direction, Israel divided his essay into its various parts, ready to address them one at a time. The first was *my home and my family,* which he wrote on the second line. I told him we skip a line between the title and the first paragraph. He crumpled the paper and threw it on the floor before beginning anew on a clean sheet. I watched him write the title on the first line, skip a line, and write *"my home and family."* Making a note to include capitalization basics in one of our lessons, I was surprised; Israel was a good speller.

He finished the word *family*, his big brown eyes full of anticipation as he sat waiting for me to tell him what to write.

"What?" he said.

"What do you mean, 'what?'"

"What do I do now?"

"You describe your home and family, just like it says," I said.

He began to tell me about his family.

"Write it down just as you say it."

His essay started to take shape.

> *I have a mother and a father and a brother we live in south phoenix my brother and me we don't get along good he is always telling me ...*

"Time out," I said. "This is your story, not your brother's. They don't care what your brother did. Plus, you haven't used any end punctuation, which makes your story confusing." We looked at sentences.

"They have two parts, a person or thing and what they did or were: We live in South Phoenix period."

I showed him a page from the AA magazine we were reading in class. Every sentence ended with a period. He registered pure amazement.

"Why would you put a dot after your sentence? That don't make no sense."

"We put the period there *as a guide to make it easier to read*. Do you know what they call that in England?" I asked. "It's called a full stop. That's a better sign of the end of something, isn't it? *We live in South Phoenix.* Period. Full Stop."

"Ohh." He proceeded to put periods at the end of his sentences and read them back to me. "I have a mother and a father and a brother stop. We live in south phoenix stop." He got it! He cabled the rest of his exit papers to me until he had about half of his essay written.

David's Condo

Meanwhile, David continued to go to Scottsdale three times a week for dialysis. On Mondays, Wednesdays, and Fridays, he returned to his apartment exhausted. On the other days, he was too tired to do more than listen to his books and nap. His mood dipped toward depression, but he managed to stay positive. Through all the vicissitudes of his health, David remained a presence. He could fill an empty room.

The VA administration finally came through with David's disability approval. To settle the claim, they issued a check for $25,000 and a monthly income larger than mine. Relieved, I almost cried.

We looked at several condos, but they were too dark, too chopped into little rooms, too expensive, whatever. Finally, our realtor took us to a little community, not far from downtown, around a small lake. When we got inside, we delighted in the open floorplan and decided we could paint the dark walls and remove the old carpet. As we were about to make an offer on it, the realtor said, "Wait, there's another one just coming on the market."

We went about three condos down to find a man putting a for-sale sign in the window. The interior open floorplan included white walls, no painting necessary. David had no credit established, so we decided I would "buy" the condo, and he would pay for it. His low mood lifted.

Twice, David visited our cousin Martha in Alaska. She established a dialysis connection with a local facility and delivered him faithfully. On the off days, they did touristy things: Denali, short cruises, and sight-seeing.

During his second return trip to Arizona, David had a heart attack and was hospitalized in Las Vegas. I was in Texas. The next day, Colleen flew to Las Vegas to accompany him on his flight back to Phoenix.

While he continued the crushing dialysis, David started to tailor the condo to his needs. Before he moved in, he replaced the worn carpet with a laminate floor, virtually indestructible and perfect for wheelchair traffic. He removed the dated white tile at the entrance and replaced it with slate. We furnished the condo sparsely, and when I moved back to Texas from Phoenix, I placed my guestroom furniture into the condo's second bedroom so I'd be able to live there if I had to.

David's health was up and down, mostly down. Each time I returned to Texas, Colleen took up the slack, hurrying to get him to the emergency room, not just several times but many times. I visited often for longer periods, but driving to Phoenix from East Texas took two days. I couldn't always get there in time.

Once I called my friends Ruth and Tom to go to the VA hospital to see about David. It was on a Saturday night when no doctors were around. David was spiking a fever, but the nurse told him she couldn't give him aspirin. The doctor on call did not want to be disturbed. I was ready to call 911 to get him out of the hospital to take him to an ER when Ruth and Tom went to the VA and talked to the nurse in charge. Tom was a retired Air Force pilot, another Viet Nam vet. I don't know what they said, but David got a call from the doctor and meds to reduce his fever. Crisis averted.

David jumped at a chance to learn home dialysis. The government supported a new initiative to teach patients to administer the treatment to themselves. He signed up and went to Scottsdale every day to learn the procedure. Medicare provided installation of reverse osmosis water and dialysis equipment into the condo.

Medicare required a person to go through the training with him. We tried a couple of people who didn't work out. To keep the training going, I stayed in Phoenix awhile and pretended to go through the training myself. I had no intention of staying there, and I certainly didn't want to study the intricacies of the circulatory system. David had the situation in hand. When the time came, he could tell me what to do so I didn't have to remember all the steps. I was never good at science and didn't want to accept the responsibility for his life-or-death dialysis. Then Trisha entered the picture. A long-time friend of mine, she was retired and looking for a part-time job. She stepped in, passed the training course, and worked for him until he died.

Trisha took care of David during the day, and Colleen continued to take him to the ER at all hours. I knew she was finding it difficult to conduct her business and take care of him, so I started spending more time in Phoenix. Toward the end, David was losing ground fast. An infection on his remaining foot turned to gangrene, requiring a regular visit from a nurse at the wound clinic. He became more incapacitated.

We still had fun together, but it was a darker time. We discovered the Italian deli down the street or brought home a lot of Chinese takeout. There were about a thousand NCIS reruns on television, and we watched them all at least once.

"Elizabeth, I'm tired," he said.

"I know," I said. "Are you tired of fighting?"

"No." He sat straighter. "I'll fight until I die." His training in special ops had created this warrior.

In the small hours of the morning, David and I did some soul searching. He asked me what my friend Ruth, a psychologist, thought about the hereafter. I said I thought she was like me and hoped to God there was one.

"There is life after death," he said resolutely. "I know it." He didn't tell me how he knew, and I didn't ask.

As David's time grew short, he assured me he would not have his foot amputated to get rid of the gangrene. "I'm not willing to let go of one more bit of quality of life," he said. I agreed to help him all I could. In one of his hospital stays, his doctor argued for amputation. David was steadfast. "No!"

The doctor pushed on, "You know what this means, don't you?"

"I know exactly what it means," David said.

Exasperated, the doctor said, "I don't want my death rate to increase."

I stepped into the conversation. "This is not about you," I said. "David said *no*, and that's good enough for me. If you take his foot off when I'm not here, I will sue you, not the hospital. YOU!"

Today I am so grateful David could make his own decisions.

One late night, he said, "Elizabeth, if you weren't here, I'd have to be in a nursing home."

"That's not going to happen, David," I assured him. "I have closed my house in Texas, and I'm here for the long haul."

Visibly shaken, he said, "I'll never be able to repay you."

"David, would you do this for me?" I said.

"You know I would."

"Enough said."

At the end of the last hospitalization, David requested to die at home. At 3:00 P.M., Ruth recommended a hospice. In a rush, they provided a new hospital bed, medications, and a nurse to greet us when we arrived back at the condo. His doctors weren't sure David could survive the trip, but he was alive, if unconscious, when we arrived. The nurse showed Trisha and me how to administer the morphine and fentanyl medication.

"I don't think he'll last the night," she said.

Trisha and I went to bed, she in my room and I in the old hospital bed next to David. At 3:00 A.M., I woke. I knew he was dead before I looked. I could feel nothing but a void; there was no David presence. Numb, I woke Trisha and called the nurse. The rest is a bad dream.

My Great Grandbabies

Connor, I have almost exhausted my tale of things I wanted to share with you and the rest of my great grandchildren. I will make one last offering: to let you all know how precious you are and how very much you mean to me.

Connor

When your mother was born, she was my "first baby" – after your grandmother, of course. And then when you came along, you became my "first new baby." I loved the whole idea of you! Early on, your parents often brought you by my house and then went to a restaurant for dinner. You and I played awhile; then I put you in the sink and bathed you, so you'd be ready for bed when you got home. When you learned to talk, your main request at my house was "chockwit." At three, you learned to stir up your own chockwit milk.

One day when you were not quite three, you wandered into my guestroom. Almost immediately you ran out of there. Wondering what scared you, I went in and looked around. You had seen my metal sculpture of a cat.

You were a happy and well-adjusted child. Children, especially boys, are seldom serene, but that adjective describes you. You never cried when your mom left you with me, and you greeted all who dropped by while you were at my house. I've told you often about taking you, aged two, to the catfish restaurant at Lake Stryker. You sat in the highchair and ate your French fries and catfish. When we left, I put you on the floor while I paid the bill. You went to every table and told the people goodbye. You've always been sweet.

At age five, one day you and I were in the pool. I said, "Connor! You're going to start school!"

"I know it," you said.

"What are you going to learn?"

"I don't know."

"Are you going to learn to read?"

"I already know how to read."

"Are you going to learn how to write?"

"I already know how to write."

"Are you going to learn arithmetic?"

"What's that?" you asked.

"That's when you hold up two fingers and you add two more fingers, so you have four fingers."

"Oh," you said. "My numbers. I already know my numbers."

"Well," I said. "I guess you can omit school and start your career."

Through your childhood years, I loved scratching your back. For hours we watched television, I, scratching and tickling your back, and you, shifting positions to get the whole back scratched. I began to call you my lizard, lying up on a rock, loving life.

You're a teenager now and still one of the kindest people I know. Your care for your siblings and cousins brings me to tears sometimes, such as the end of the first day of school, when you got off the bus because Bendi was not there. The bus took off without you, and you went to find Bendi. Being new to the school, she had missed the bus. You called your mom and waited until Kiss came to the school to get you both.

My wish for you is health, happiness, and prosperity in your life. It has been an honor to be your great grandmother.

Bendi

I became the luckiest grandmother in the world when you were born! Your family lived with me, and I got all the rocking-chair time I wanted. I showed your mom and dad how to bathe a newborn; we fixed bottles together; and I learned all over again how to change diapers! When your daddy was at work and your mama was at the college, you stayed with me. We played and read books.

When you were tiny, I could let you grasp my fingers and pull you up to a sitting position, saying, "Come on, come on..." You were the strongest baby I had ever seen. You learned early to drink through a straw and drain my glass of lemon-water. And when you were about to cry, you pursed your lips in the cutest, funniest way.

You walked at nine months! I had a hard time keeping up with you. One day before your first birthday, you exited the house and were toddling toward the street before I found you. As a baby, you often climbed up to the arm of the red leather sofa and dived off headfirst. You kept me on my toes. Jo Carol and I took you to the Thompson family reunion when you were a year old. You ran behind the older children, trying to keep up. It was so cute to see a baby in a diaper running along behind the other toddlers.

Every Wednesday, I took you to the "libarry," where you got a helium balloon and a costume. The librarian read a children's story, sometimes to a room full of kids. You'd come back home costumed as a honeybee or some other animal, always with a balloon flying high.

Too soon you had to leave Jacksonville and me, moving to Las Cruces with your daddy. I felt such pain and loneliness when you left, but I loved your large, happy family in New Mexico. I knew you were loved. And you visited us here in Texas as often as possible. At times, I drove through Las Cruces on my way to Phoenix, stopping overnight to visit with you and your daddy.

Once I took you with me to Phoenix. On the long, hot trip you paid attention when we went through little towns in eastern Arizona.

"Nana, a park!" you exclaimed, and we stopped for a little while to play on the swings. In Phoenix, we played with the water hose in the warm mornings, watched "Bewitched" and "I Dream of Jeanie" in the hot afternoons, and went to the playground in the park in the cooler evenings. We had so much fun together.

You often said things to make me laugh. When you were about seven, you were demonstrating to Maddison, Daisy, and Brandon how to play "The farmer in the *deli*. High, ho, the merry-oh! The farmer in the *deli*." Then your game took a turn toward the macabre. "The farmer takes a life," you sang. I have entertained my friends with this story.

There are times when my arms ache to hold you again, my tiny baby. But you've grown into a beautiful girl, pretty inside and out. Of all my children, so far you have become the best reader. You could read comments off the television screen when you were eight as well as any adult. And you immediately comprehended the magic in the book *December* by Eve Bunting.

This year you moved back to Texas. *O happy day!* You go to the same school as your cousins and ride the same bus home in the afternoons. You've already made good friends and are doing well here. I know you miss your Tia in New Mexico; I wish you could have both families close by.

My wish for you is a long life, complete with the knowledge of how strong and wise you are.

You are smart, kind, and thoughtful, and I'm so proud of you.

Maddison

What can I say about you, Maddison? You are so much like your mama when she was a child. Her wit was quick, and she wasn't shy about saying what was on her mind, a wonderful quality. That's how I experience you.

When you were four, you spent a day at my house. You devised a game for us to play. You took all my emery boards from my desk drawer and some plastic letters in all colors from the refrigerator. Your game was "popsicle store." For hours, we bought and sold popsicles. The letters were the different colored popsicles while the emery boards were the money. We took turns being the lady who sold and the lady who bought.

I asked several times, "Can we stop now?"

"No," you said as you began a new round of buying and selling.

You are so creative. I have loved your painting of trees on my wall. I hung it so it would show in the background in my Zoom classes. Several people have remarked on it. You made my initials in plastic, and several pieces of art I've hung on my fridge.

I brag to my friends about your expertise in barrel racing. When I told one of them you won a belt buckle, he said, "Nine-year-olds compete against older kids! Quite an accomplishment." About six weeks ago, you won second in the world competition, reserve champion! Another belt buckle, a jacket, and $900 in scholarships. Wow! I'm so impressed.

You also make me laugh! Your rules for Dylan's room are hilarious. You probably didn't see the irony of making rules for his room when you bunked in with him. Your requirements for him in *his* room were bossy. My favorite was the last one, "Call me Queen Maddison!" Did he?

As you grow, your personality becomes more distinct. You have an innate sense of justice, instantly running to the defense of an underdog. I admire that about you; you are fair in your dealings with everyone around you. And you run a tight ship with your brothers, requiring them to behave themselves.

Dylan

You are a most wonderful child! As a baby, you were contented with whatever and wherever. One day when you were about a year old, your mom kept you in your car seat in her truck when she made some deliveries to Trinity Church. They were having an annual garage sale, and your mom was delivering some big items to be sold.

The priest, Father Godwin, and your mother worked to get rugs and other items into the parish hall. They stood around the truck, talking for a long time. After a while, Father Godwin looked inside the truck and exclaimed, "I had no idea there was a baby in there." He was amazed at how calm and patient you were.

I had to agree with him. You were happy every time I saw you. And then you turned three years old! On the day after your birthday, you came into the house with a rubber ball in your hand.

"What have you got?" I asked.

Instead of answering, you threw the ball at me and hit me in the face.

A worker bee, you are the child we count on to pitch in to help. What a glorious attribute! You love to walk my dog out front. She, of course, loves that, too. You get her to do her tricks for treats and generally entertain yourself when you visit. You're still calm, cool, and collected. I admire your ethic. You're so smart and a joy to be around.

BEN

You spent your first three years in Colorado, so I didn't get to know you till you moved to Texas, but you were worth waiting for! When I asked you what something meant, you said, "I do not know what that is." You didn't use *don't* or other contractions, and your terrible allergies stuffed your nose, so your reply sounded like, "I do dot doe..." It made me laugh!

You fit right in with our family and in my heart. Not shy at all, you were always there to give me a hug, to talk to me, and to ask lots of questions. Your sweetness reminded me of Connor when he was your age.

When you turned five years old, I said, "Ben! You're going to go to school!"

You said, "I doe it!"

"What are you going to learn?" I asked.

"I do dot doe," you said.

"Are you going to learn to read?"

"I hope so!" [My favorite indicator of your eagerness to learn.]

"Are you going to learn to write?"

"I already doe how to write," you assured me.

"Are you going to learn arithmetic?" I asked.

"I do dot doe what that is."

While I explained what arithmetic is, you lost interest in the conversation and wandered off.

You are our only child who likes veggies, a diet promising a long and healthy life for you. You always run to me when you see me. You hug and tell me you love me. That's worth all the gold in the world. I'm so glad you're my great grandson.

www.ingramcontent.com/pod-product-compliance
Lightning Source LLC
Chambersburg PA
CBHW020903080526
44589CB00011B/419